A Scholar's Guide to Getting Published in English

Full details of all our publications can be found on
http://www.multilingual-matters.com, or by writing to
Multilingual Matters, St Nicholas House,
31-34 High Street, Bristol BS1 2AW, UK.

A Scholar's Guide to Getting Published in English

Critical Choices and Practical Strategies

Mary Jane Curry and Theresa Lillis

MULTILINGUAL MATTERS
Bristol • Buffalo • Toronto

Library of Congress Cataloging in Publication Data
A catalog record for this book is available from the Library of Congress.
Curry, Mary Jane.
A Scholar's Guide to Getting Published in English: Critical Choices and Practical Strategies/
Mary Jane Curry and Theresa Lillis.
Includes bibliographical references and index.
1. Authorship. 2. Academic writing. 3. Scholarly publishing. 4. Scholarly periodicals--
Publishing. I. Lillis, Theresa M.- II. Title.
PN146.C87 2014
808.02–dc23 2013023704

British Library Cataloguing in Publication Data
A catalogue entry for this book is available from the British Library.

ISBN-13: 978-1-78309-060-0 (hbk)
ISBN-13: 978-1-78309-059-4 (pbk)

Multilingual Matters
UK: St Nicholas House, 31-34 High Street, Bristol BS1 2AW, UK.
USA: UTP, 2250 Military Road, Tonawanda, NY 14150, USA.
Canada: UTP, 5201 Dufferin Street, North York, Ontario M3H 5T8, Canada.

The policy of Multilingual Matters/Channel View Publications is to use papers that are
natural, renewable and recyclable products, made from wood grown in sustainable forests.
In the manufacturing process of our books, and to further support our policy, preference is
given to printers that have FSC and PEFC Chain of Custody certification. The FSC and/or
PEFC logos will appear on those books where full certification has been granted to the
printer concerned.

Text design and typesetting by John Maggs Design Ltd, Corsham.
Printed and bound in Great Britain by Lavenham Press Ltd.

Contents

List of Information Boxes

List of Figures

Acknowledgements

We wish to thank all the scholars who have generously given their time, texts, thoughts and interest in the decade-plus that we have worked on the research that informs this guide and our earlier publications from the project.

We are grateful to the following for feedback during the development of this guide: participants at a workshop at the 2011 Second Language Writing Symposium in Taipei, Taiwan; scholars at the Technological Institute of Monterrey, Mexico; scholars at Chuo University in Japan; members of Mary Jane Curry's First Friday Group doctoral seminar, particularly for the assistance of Lisa Metzger; other students and colleagues at the Warner Graduate School of Education and Human Development at the University of Rochester; and members of the Academic Literacies Group at the Open University. We wish to thank Pamela Kaptein and Christopher Penders at the University of Rochester for help in preparing the text. The research on which this project is based has been funded by our respective universities, the Economic and Social Research Council (RES-000-22-0098 and RES-063-27-0263) and the British Academy.

Permission is gratefully acknowledged to reprint or adapt the following: To *TESOL Quarterly* for: Curry, M.J. and Lillis, T.M. (2004) Multilingual scholars and the imperative to publish in English: Negotiating interests, demands, and rewards. *TESOL Quarterly* 38 (4), 663-688. To *Revista Canaria de Estudios Ingleses* for: Lillis, T.M. and Curry, M.J. (2006) Reframing notions of competence in scholarly writing: From individual to networked activity. *Revista Canaria de Estudios Ingleses* 53, 63-78. To Taylor & Francis for extracts from pages 69, 132 and 139 of: Lillis, T.M. and Curry, M.J. (2010) *Academic Writing in a Global Context: The Politics and Practices of Publishing in English.* London: Routledge. Extracts from the *Learning & Instruction* website used by permission. Copyright Elsevier 2013. To the American Psychological Association for extracts from the *Psychological Review* website. To Andria Wisler and Celina del Felice for extracts from the call for book chapters.

Our ongoing love and thanks to our families who have supported us in this long journey: to Moritz, Rumpole, Guille, Carmen, and Liam.

Introduction

'Publish or perish' is a familiar mantra in academia, one heard among discussions of academics' multiple responsibilities for teaching, working with undergraduate and postgraduate students and providing institutional administrative service. In many locations around the globe we can now add the words 'in English' to this well-worn slogan, as many scholars are coming under increasing pressure to publish in English, alongside or instead of publishing in their local/national language or other languages. In addition to scholars' personal interests in publishing in various outlets (and languages), academic institutions and governments around the world are increasingly making it imperative for scholars to publish in English, particularly in what are considered to be high-status 'international' journals that are included in particular journal or citation indexes. As well, in an era of increased global mobility of scholars, post-graduate students and even institutions (as, for example, in the case of 'satellite' campuses of UK- and US-based universities in other regions of the world), the role of English in academia more broadly is growing.

In this guide we therefore take as our starting position that while most scholarly activity around the world involves multilingual activity, it is taking place in a global context which increasingly sets a premium on using – and publishing in – English. Scholars are grappling with considerable demands, often with limited time and restricted resources. They face complex decisions about where and how to direct their research and writing activity. This situation affects scholars from Anglophone and non-Anglophone contexts differently. For scholars based in Anglophone-centre contexts[1], decisions about which language to publish in are often viewed as straightforward – English. Yet for many scholars working in and through several languages on

1

a daily basis, making decisions about which languages to use can be a crucial and challenging aspect to their publishing activity.

The main goal of this guide is to offer guidance, information and practical suggestions to anyone seeking to publish or to support others to publish, but it is oriented in particular toward scholars who are living and writing outside of Anglophone contexts and who are seeking to publish in English in addition to other languages. Some scholars will see writing and publishing in English as central to their intellectual and professional goals, even though it may add to their workloads. For other scholars publishing in English may mean taking time away from key commitments and interests, such as writing in their local/national or in other languages for communities other than those addressed by English-medium 'international' journals (see Chapter 1). For all scholars, understanding the social practices of journal publishing may help in making critical choices about how to spend their limited time and energy. In addition, current fast-paced changes to the practices of scholarly publishing, for example, through the rise of online access to academic publications – are affecting not only the nature of 'scholarly journals' but also submission, review and publication practices. The topic of open access journals is hotly debated as on the one hand holding potential for the dissemination of academic knowledge in a world with vastly uneven distribution of resources, and on the other hand presenting an opportunity for what Beall (2013) calls 'predatory' open access publishers who aim to profit by charging individual scholars large sums to publish their papers. The open-access debate is one of the key areas that scholars may want to monitor and participate in.

Key assumptions driving this guide

While many experienced scholars are familiar with their local publishing contexts, the imperative to publish in English as well as in other languages can present new considerations and challenges. And of course, added to this, acceptance rates in what are considered to be high-status English-medium journals are discouragingly low for all scholars, including authors who work in English only. Publishing in English-medium journals often involves becoming familiar with new practices, thus layering on additional demands for scholars who are already successful in local and regional contexts and presenting challenges to those relatively new to writing for publication. Key challenges include: identifying the most appropriate journal(s) to target for the submission of particular texts; coming to understand a range of editorial and practices according to different contexts; making connections and forging collaborations with other scholars locally and transnationally; working with people who can 'broker' access to publishing, or support multilingual drafting and text production in different ways (i. e. through editing or translating); and responding to diverse communication and feedback practices from journal editors and reviewers across different contexts.

This guide's approach to supporting writing for publication

Proficiency in particular languages (including English) and facility with academic writing are clearly important to scholars' publishing success. However, a body of research (including our own) has demonstrated that individual English proficiency alone is not always the key to achieving success in English-medium publishing. In this guide we therefore take a different approach to supporting scholars in journal article publishing than that taken by most other books on writing for publication. Rather than focus mainly on the linguistic and rhetorical strategies involved in scholarly writing for publication, this guide aims to help scholars explore the larger social practices, politics, networks and resources involved in academic publishing and to encourage scholars to consider how they wish to take part in these practices – as well as to engage in current debates about them. The book is intended to complement available linguistic and rhetorical guides to writing for publication, some important examples of which are noted as useful resources in chapters of this guide (key examples being Belcher, 2009; Murray, 2009; Paltridge & Starfield, in press; Swales & Feak 2009, 2011).

The notion of 'social practices' is central to our understanding of what's involved in academic writing for publication and underpins our approach in this guide. Academic writing as social practice reflects a recognition that:

• the ways that people do things often become part of their implicit routines or habitual patterns of activity;

• the expectations accompanying these patterns vary according to the specific contexts in which they take place;

- practices are tied to institutions and structures that involve power dynamics and specific ideologies related to knowledge production and language(s) – including about English; and

- practices are ever-evolving in response to personal, institutional, local contextual and global influences.

The social practices of scholarly publishing include: participating in projects that can lead to presenting and publishing research; negotiating collaborations on projects and texts; attending conferences and participating in networks both at conferences and in other locations; choosing an appropriate target journal for a particular paper; drafting papers to address the interests and conversations of a particular journal; and understanding and responding to feedback from gatekeepers and others. Woven throughout all of these practices are the geolinguistic power dynamics that affect the availability of research funding and other resources and types of access to means of research dissemination for scholars around the world (Canagarajah, 2002; Flowerdew, 1999a, 1999b, 2000; Lillis & Curry, 2010; Salager-Meyer, 1997, 2008).

A key goal of this guide is to support scholars' publishing goals by helping scholars to identify and understand the practices of academic publishing, particularly – but not exclusively – in English, and to encourage scholars to make best use of the available resources to support publishing. An important related strand across the guide points up tensions that may arise between scholars' personal interests in, and institutional pressures for, publishing in English and scholars' personal commitments and interests in publishing in local, regional or other languages. The guide aims to connect scholars' existing knowledge of publishing practices with their interests in publishing in English. By focusing on publishing in terms of practices, institutions and politics – rather than on language and writing alone – this guide aims to:

- support readers in understanding what is entailed and at stake in taking on various publishing roles in multiple communities;

- raise readers' awareness of current global debates and issues related to the different kinds of publishing and scholarly activity; and

- involve readers in these debates – including key tensions – and how scholars might work to challenge or transform some of these pressures and tensions.

Whilst this guide focuses principally on scholars as authors, we also recognize that at different moments in their working lives scholars take up various roles associated with publishing practices and we try to signal some of the benefits and challenges of taking on these roles: most obviously we point to the roles of collaborator/co-author, manuscript reviewer and journal editor. As Chapter 1 discusses, scholars may engage in a range of communities (local, regional, transnational), with a range of audiences (academic, applied) and in a range of languages (e.g. local/national, English, other).

Positioning ourselves as writers, imagining our readers

We are writing this guide from the position of scholars living and working in Anglophone-centre contexts (Curry in the United States and Lillis in the United Kingdom) who are aware of the privileges that these global locations currently bestow – whilst at the same time being aware of differences in opportunity and access within the 'centre' as well as between and within contexts sometimes called 'peripheral', most obviously in terms of the use of English. We consider that many of the practices of writing for academic publishing are hidden or opaque and involve ideologies that discriminate against some scholars more than others. We are committed to contributing to ways of working toward greater and more equal access to academic publishing by scholars around the world.

In writing this guide, we have imagined two main types of reader: 'the reader' as an individual scholar looking for information and support for writing for publication, and 'the reader' as someone working to support others' publishing activity, such as a teacher/supervisor/advisor, a more senior colleague, an academic writing specialist or a language consultant working with teams of researchers or journal editorial boards. The chapters are intended to function as a resource to be used or modified according to the specific context and interests of the reader. Thus whilst across the guide we use 'you' to address individual scholars to encourage reflection on individual circumstances, we also assume that the publishing activities we discuss may be mediated by others.

Whether used by individual scholars or by professionals who are supporting scholars, we consider this guide may be relevant to scholars at different stages in their working lives. So, for example, because in many contexts postgraduate students are increasingly encouraged or required to publish before they finish their degrees, this guide will be useful for supporting students. At the same time it will be useful for experienced scholars seeking to publish in less familiar contexts. In trialing the chapters in this guide we found that both more and less experienced scholars from a range of contexts – including Anglophone centre and non-Anglophone contexts – have considered its ideas and activities relevant to their situations and interests.[2]

Where the ideas, principles and examples in this guide come from

This guide draws on our extensive research on multilingual scholars' experiences with English-medium publishing in a global context, Professional Academic Writing in a Global Context[3] (PAW; Curry & Lillis, 2004, 2010a; Lillis & Curry, 2006a, 2006b, 2010, 2013), as well as broader debates about academic publishing. Our empirical research has explored the writing and publishing practices of education and psychology scholars in southern and central Europe, with a specific focus on publishing in English. We wanted to understand scholars' experiences over time in writing and submitting their academic work, the tensions and conflicts they experience as they respond to the pressure to publish (in English) and their perspectives on the growing dominance of English in global publishing.

We call our research approach 'text-ethnographic,' meaning that we explore the production of academic texts for publication as taking place within particular social contexts (Lillis, 2008; Lillis & Curry 2006a). To do so we have been involved in wide-ranging data collection since 2001, including: field notes made in 60 visits to scholars located in 12 institutions across four national contexts – Hungary, Slovakia, Spain and Portugal; the collection of approximately 1200 texts written by scholars and 500 copies of correspondence about texts between participants and others (e.g. colleagues, reviewers, editors); some 250 text-based interviews with scholars; and considerable documentary data from academic departments and institutions as well as national policy documents. One of our key means of analysing the project data has been the (re)construction of what we call 'text histories', sets of data such as interviews, field notes, scholars' writings and their correspondence with journal gatekeepers, which we have analysed to help us understand the trajectory of texts toward publication (or not). Full details of the data and the project findings are discussed in *Academic writing in a global context: The politics and practices of English-medium publishing* (Lillis & Curry, 2010). Key points arising from our research have particularly influenced us in writing this guide:

1. There is increasing pressure on scholars around the world to publish in English. Many scholars are publishing multilingually – even as they work to publish in English. Writing for publication often involves others, including people we call 'literacy brokers', who act as a social resource crucial to publishing in scholarly journals (Lillis & Curry, 2006a; 2010). In addition, literacy brokers, as well as others, often form part of a scholar's academic research networks, a resource that can be central to publishing success (Curry & Lillis, 2010a).

2. A key challenge is often accessing appropriate or relevant resources. These material resources include funding for research (e.g. for equipment, materials, assistance, release time), library resources such as subscriptions to journals, funding for travel to conferences to present research and participate in academic research networks, and support in text production (including for language brokers such as copyeditors and translators, journal page fees). Limited resources for these aspects of conducting and disseminating research can place many multilingual scholars at a clear disadvantage. In addition, in many places there are few workshops or courses on academic publishing available, thus scholars often have little information about publication practices (see Canagarajah, 1996; Mweru, 2010).

This guide is based on the extensive ethnographic data we have collected for over a decade. We include a small amount of data we have discussed in our previous publications but the majority of the data we use here is newly analysed and has not been previously published. We are of course also aware of research by other scholars on the topic of academic publishing, much of which has been conducted in other regions of the world and with scholars across a number of disciplines. Therefore, in each chapter we include a section that lists some of the research from other contexts that relates to the focus of each of this guide's chapters (see Key Tools, p. 11).

As with our research publications, in this guide we take pains not to compromise confidentiality about scholars' identities. To do this we use pseudonyms and in some cases we withhold information such as national contexts or disciplines; in addition, in presenting data we typically remove information from text extracts that would identify the sub-fields in which scholars work. We use square brackets [ ] in data extracts to indicate the omitted material. Our transcriptions of scholars' talk use standard orthography and we cut repetitions and hesitancies of speech. Being aware of debates on the politics of representation (Bucholtz, 2000; Roberts, 1997), we aim to find a position between accuracy of representation and providing a flavour of scholars' expression in English, whilst avoiding stigmatising multilingual scholars as 'non-native' users of English.

Labels and categories

The labels and categories used to discuss what is involved in academic writing for publication are fraught with complications. Terms such as 'national', 'international', 'local' and 'global' are not fixed in meaning and often take on different connotations depending on where scholars are situated globally. To take an obvious example, an 'international journal' may not simply mean – as the phrase implies – a journal with authors or an editorial board from around the world, but may rather signal a journal with a particular status (high), or a journal with an 'impact factor', and, often, a journal publishing in the medium of English (see Lillis & Curry, 2010). In writing this guide we have tried to use these terms both in 'common sense' ways in order to inform readers about current uses and practices, but also to problematise them by indicating their contested nature. We also use less common terms such as 'transnational' to signal that scholars are writing for a range of communities (see Chapter 1) rather than using any seemingly straightforward mapping of specific languages against 'local', 'national' or 'international' communities. We aim to indicate that scholars are writing for particular audiences/communities that use particular languages for specific reasons. For example, in a number of contexts, English-medium publications may or may not be addressed to predominantly Anglophone audiences in centre locations.

In referring to languages that scholars use we also avoid using the terms L1 (first language) and L2 (second language) or 'native' and 'nonnative', recognizing that:

- scholars' personal histories are particular and often complex, so that, for example, the assumption that Portuguese is the first or primary language of all scholars from Portugal is neither likely to be accurate nor reflective of the mobility (real and virtual) of scholars in contemporary times; and

- terms such as 'L1/L2', 'native' and 'nonnative' tend to be used evaluatively and are unhelpful when attempting to describe and account for the actual social practices of academic writing.

Instead we use terms that signal the geopolitical and relational position of languages with regard to academic publishing: we therefore use the term 'local/national' language to contrast a language that a scholar may be using in her everyday lifeworld – such as a scholar living and working in Hungary using Hungarian – with her use of other languages, such as 'English', which the same scholar may also be using, more or less regularly, as part of her academic work. Furthermore, our preference for 'local/national' to refer to language(s) used in everyday contexts signals our understanding that a local language may or may not be the same as a national language, so, for example, the nation state of Spain recognizes official languages in addition to Castilian (Catalan, Galician, etc.); similarly, the Hungarian language is used by a minority of Slovak citizens in Slovakia.[4]

Furthermore, although we use the label 'English' in a seemingly simplistic way throughout the guide, we also recognize that there are multiple forms of English, both those considered 'standard' (e.g. Canadian, British, American, Australian) and those considered as 'World Englishes' or varieties of English used in contexts where other languages have historically been dominant. In this guide we do not discuss this range of Englishes in relation to academic publication, but rather foreground the status of 'English'-medium publications in general and signal the differential status of 'English-medium' according to context of publication.

The genres the guide covers – and why

This guide focus primarily on practices related to academic journal article publishing, with some discussion of book chapters; we do not discuss the publishing of whole books, book reviews, grant applications, reports or other academic genres. Although in some disciplines and some contexts the publishing of books is an important form of research dissemination and therefore of professional evaluation, in many academic areas book publishing is not as highly valued as is journal article publishing. Rather, the refereed scholarly journal article is a genre that garners high status in many academic and governmental reward systems.[5] In many disciplines journal publications function as the primary 'currency' of academia, playing a key role in building scholars' reputations and in institutional decisions to hire, promote, and tenure scholars as well as for research funding. Edited book chapters can be similar to journal articles in scope and length. However, key differences exist: the content and structure of book chapters tend to differ from those of journal articles; the process of contributing a book chapter differs from that of submitting to a journal; and book chapters often carry less status than do refereed journal articles in evaluation criteria. Thus while we recognize that book publishing plays a role in research dissemination, in this guide we focus primarily on journal articles, with some attention to book chapters as a similar, but not identical, genre.

The academic disciplines discussed in this guide

The PAW study that forms the basis of this guide involves scholars in the areas of education and psychology. However, many of their experiences as social scientists resonate with what our informal communications with scholars in other fields tell us about the pressures on academics. Indeed, research shows that while some academic writing and publishing practices in other disciplines differ from those of the social sciences (and that there is variation within social sciences), many of the choices and strategies we present in this guide will be relevant to scholars and postgraduates in many disciplines. Furthermore, some of the studies we include in the section 'Related research' in each chapter of this guide examine scholarship from other academic disciplines.

Key tools: heuristics for understanding writing for publication

In this guide we draw on research findings to offer a series of *heuristics* for making visible the choices that scholars make and the strategies they adopt, in order to encourage readers to consider their own choices and strategies. Heuristics are frameworks for identifying, exploring and potentially solving problems which seek to be meaningful to people's experiences and goals without falling into easy prescriptivism (Curry & Lillis, 2010b). Throughout the guide we invite readers to consider issues, themes, questions and decisions raised by scholars in our study and to consider how they might be relevant to their experiences and circumstances. By introducing readers to authentic examples and text histories we hope to make visible the practices of writing for academic publication, the critical choices scholars make and the practical strategies they adopt. Although we aim to avoid a prescriptive stance, we do offer guidance and advice, sometimes adopting a didactic tone (most clearly in directing readers' attention to data extracts): but our main goal is to encourage discussion and informed decision making.

The heuristics consist of data examples and analyses, followed by sets of questions to help readers to link key points in each chapter with their own experiences and dilemmas. By basing each chapter's heuristics on data about, and accounts of, scholars' practices, we aim to show variation in scholars' situations so that readers can contemplate the issues raised rather than receiving potentially irrelevant instructions. Chapters are addressed to readers in the second person and include these key elements:

- **Chapter focus** – a discussion of the main focus which arises from research findings and is connected to the research data presented in the next section;

- **Data, questions and comment** – research data that support reflection and, for readers working with others, discussion about the chapter focus, such as artifacts (e.g. institutional documents about how publications are rewarded, authors' publications records, extracts of texts written for publication and extracts of correspondence with journal gatekeepers), questions that prompt readers to analyze and reflect on the focus of the chapter, followed by a comment on the data and issues presented;

- **Thinking about your practice** – questions to link readers' reflections on the data to their current or future participation in the practices discussed in the chapter;

- **Suggestions for future action** – ideas for how readers might respond to the issues raised in each heuristic and learn more about the publishing practices and available resources in their contexts;

- **Useful resources** – books, articles and websites and other materials related to the focus of each chapter;

- **Related research** – other scholarship on the topic of each heuristic, often from different disciplinary or regional contexts other than those represented in our data.

Each chapter ends with Information Box which includes background information about a key topic related to the focus of the chapter.

How to use this guide

This guide can be used individually for self-study or collectively in a workshop or classroom context. The order of chapters is organized broadly along a common trajectory of publishing processes and timelines. Because key aspects of publishing are clearly interrelated, we often make cross-references to other chapters and Information Boxes. We view academic publishing as the public face of knowledge production, that is, as one of the multiple ways that scholars interact with the world, their disciplinary subject matter and their personal and political commitments. Thus the guide begins by inviting readers to consider the reasons for publishing various types of texts, the range of communities they write for and the pressures, challenges and opportunities of academic publishing. The first chapter asks readers to reflect on their personal and political commitments and how they might inform decisions about academic publishing, including responses to institutional, governmental or other pressures to publish in various languages. The second chapter explores how some of these institutional and governmental pressures to publish are codified in official documents in different contexts. In the third chapter we invite readers to examine how scholars respond to interests in and pressures to publish in certain communities.

Chapters 4 to 6 take up what Bazerman (1980) calls the 'organized conversations of academic disciplines' to explore how to identify and contribute to current topics, discussions and debates taking place in conferences and journals in a discipline/disciplinary area. Identifying these conversations can help readers make strategic decisions in evaluating which venues to choose as 'targets' for article manuscripts. Chapter 7 focuses on how citation practices are implicated in contributing to these conversations and locating one's work in the academic landscape. Next, Chapter 8 considers a choice that many scholars face – whether to publish journal articles or chapters in edited books. It examines how journal articles and book chapters share some similarities (e.g. length, format) while representing certain different practices, including how book chapters are evaluated.

In Chapters 9 to 11 we turn our focus to the resources needed to support scholarly publishing, both those related to discursive aspects of publishing and those Canagarajah (1996) identifies as the 'non-discursive' requirements of publishing – starting with the fundamental resource of time; bibliographic resources which are foundational to participating in academic conversations; monetary funds needed to conduct research; funds to support translating, editing and proofreading of manuscripts; and funds for travel to conferences to present research and to make connections with other scholars in academic research networks.

Such connections may result in a range of professional relationships, which are addressed in Chapters 12 to 16: networking, collaborating, brokering and communicating with gatekeepers. Other scholars constitute one aspect of social resources, including people we call 'literacy brokers', those who are involved in the production of texts at various stages, including ultimate gatekeepers such as journal editors and reviewers. We explore the kinds of support that different types of 'literacy brokers' can offer, depending on the brokers' relationship to the academy. Throughout these chapters we invite readers to consider where to locate the kinds of resources we identify as useful and how to engage with them.

We conclude the guide with a chapter that explores some of the less commonly discussed social practices of scholarly publication. These involve taking on reviewing and editorial roles in academic journals, another important way that scholars contribute to conversations in their disciplines. Ultimately, we hope that this guide will support readers' publishing endeavors while also encouraging contributions to the ongoing debates about scholarly publishing practices in a global context.

Notes

1 We use the 'centre-periphery' distinction following World Systems theory (Wallerstein, 1991) to indicate different material circumstances and geopolitical relations of dependency between global regions.

2 In order to draw on the perspectives of multilingual scholars about the usefulness of this guide, we have presented various chapters, at different stages of development, to scholars and postgraduates at research conferences, in teaching situations and through email. We have also presented chapters to colleagues and post-graduate students at our respective institutions to solicit their views (see Acknowledgements).

3 For details of the PAW project see http://creet.open.ac.uk/projects/paw/.

4 Of course, the question of what constitutes a language is a much larger issue – a relevant example is that 'Slovak' and 'Czech' are two languages that at the same time are considered by many to be mutually intelligible.

5 Generally speaking, genre refers to a 'type' of text and how it functions according to the norms and values of particular contexts.

Chapter 1

Identifying your personal interests and commitments to publishing

1.1 **Chapter focus**

Scholars in many contexts around the world are coming under increasing pressure to publish, in English as well as in other languages, and are motivated by a range of interests and goals. At different points in their careers scholars write for different and sometimes multiple communities, depending on their goals and commitments. Scholars make decisions about which communities to address based on their priorities about the content, focus and audience for various publications. Understanding the range of reasons that scholars publish is important for considering which communities you may want to address at different moments in your academic work and career and in which language(s).

1.2 **Scholarly interests and communities**

The table in Data Example 1.1 illustrates the range of communities to which multilingual scholars contribute and the language(s) used in each community. What do you notice about the range of communities? What relationship do you see between the content and purpose of different types of publications and the languages used in publications for particular communities? Bearing in mind that any labeling of the communities that scholars write for is not straightforward, to what extent are the types of communities listed relevant to your publishing activity?

Data Example 1.1: Academic communities to which multilingual scholars contribute

Community/Language	Type of Publications
1. **National academic community in the local/ national/state language** (e.g. Spanish, Hungarian, as discussed in the Introduction)	*Scholarly publications* aimed at the national research community
2. **National applied community in local/national language**	*Practitioner publications* aimed at users of research findings such as teachers, health professionals, psychologists
3. **National academic community in English**	*Scholarly publications* often aimed at a wider audience than the audience reached by publications in the local/national language
4. **'International' academic community in the local/ national language**	*Scholarly publications* using local/national languages aimed at a wider audience than the local context (e.g. Spanish in Latin America, Portuguese in Brazil and Africa, Slovak in the Czech Republic)
5. **'Intranational' academic community in medium of English**	*Scholarly publications* aimed at a transnational or transregional audience with strong political links, such as the European Union
6. **Other national academic community in national languages**	*Scholarly publications* in languages that represent intellectual traditions related to particular (sub)fields, as well as geo-historical relations such as the role of German and Russian in central European contexts like Slovakia and Hungary
7. **'International' academic community in medium of English**	*Scholarly publications* typically produced in Anglophone contexts and distributed worldwide, which increasingly often have higher status than journals published in other parts of the world and sometimes indicated by inclusion in high status indexes and with an impact factor (see Information Boxes 1 and 2)

(For fuller discussion, see Lillis and Curry, 2010: chap. 2.)

Comment

The table indicates a number of communities that scholars are seeking to address, including research and applied or practitioner communities in local languages, English or other languages. The range of communities that scholars address changes according to historical links between communities of scholars, individual interests, and personal and academic circumstances. Some scholars, for example, write for all of the communities listed in Data Example 1.1 while some write mainly for a selection of them. While many scholars are publishing in multiple languages, the ratio of their publications using the local language as compared to other languages varies considerably. Some scholars make a distinction between communities they are writing for on the basis of the content of their texts: for example, some scholars address applied communities using the local language(s), while they contribute theoretical or research publications to 'intranational' or 'international' communities in English. In contrast, some scholars find that there are more opportunities for developing advanced theory when addressing local communities in the local/national language, because their writings are part of ongoing and well-established local research and knowledge-building activities (such as seminars at which different stages of theory and research are presented).

1.3 Making decisions about where to publish

When thinking about where to publish – and which genres of text to publish (see Introduction) – scholars take into consideration a number of factors, as one scholar's publication record across the communities discussed in Section 1.2 illustrates. Look at Data Example 1.2 and consider the following question: What does Amalia's record of publishing in these communities suggest about her interests and personal commitments?

Data Example 1.2: Publications record of Amalia, associate professor[1] of psychology, Portugal

Community	Journal articles	Book chapters	Edited Books	Books	Conference proceedings
1. National academic community in Portuguese	3	3* (2)	1	1	1
2. National applied community in Portuguese		4	1	1	
4. 'International' academic community in Portuguese	2	*			
7. 'International' academic community in English	1				

*Single-authored publication; others are co-authored or co-edited.

Comment

Amalia has published in four of the seven types of community listed in Data Example 1.2. She has published in both the local/national research and applied communities using the local language (Portuguese) and has four publications addressed to the 'international' academic community, also in the local language. Amalia has published one English-medium journal article for the 'international' community in her specialist area, which she co-authored with a colleague from Canada. In the next section we explore some of Amalia's reasons for addressing this range of communities.

1.4 **One scholar's thoughts on where to publish**

Read about the personal commitments that inform Amalia's publishing choices in Data Example 1.3 and consider the question: How do Amalia's comments support what her publications record suggests to you about her choices of communities to address through her publications?

Data Example 1.3: Views of Amalia, associate professor, Portugal, on choosing scholarly communities

'I have always preferred to know that what I am working on has some application, some use. That's why I'm working on the project with [a colleague in the education department], because we are applying our resources with people who really need that. […] That for me is important, to really do something not just theoretically.'

[…]

'There are things that maybe you want people in Portugal to know, so it will be easier if you publish that in Portuguese here … because it may be something especially from here, from this community, for example.'

[…]

'I like things that usually mean the application of research findings because then you are working on things that perhaps are of value. It seems the academic research publications are not worth so much in practical terms; they are worth something, but I do not have that goal.'

Comment

Amalia's choice of communities reflects her priorities that her academic work should have value in the local context, as the majority of her publications are aimed at local/national communities, both research and applied. Although in Amalia's context there is some institutional pressure to publish in English, other factors also influence scholars' career opportunities. Thus Amalia's publications in Portuguese as well as English have supported her to become a permanent faculty member at her university (along with her teaching and other academic responsibilities). Amalia has there-

fore been able to receive institutional recognition while following her own interests and commitments. (See Chapter 3 for different choices made by Julie, a Hungarian scholar.) Amalia's achievement indicates that in her particular context publishing in the local/national community is as valued as publishing in 'international contexts'. (See Information Box 1 on the meanings of 'international' and Chapters 2 and 3 on institutional evaluation systems.)

1.5 **Thinking about your practice**

1. What problems, topics and research questions are of most interest and importance to you?

2. Which of the communities in Data Example 1.1 have you already written for? What are your personal goals and priorities in terms of the community/ies you want to reach at the moment? To what extent do your priorities map onto those of your institutional context?

3. Are there other communities/groups you want to publish in, now or in the future? Which might these be and why are they important to you? (See Chapter 4 for discussion of communities such as online blogs, journals and websites.)

1.6 **Suggestions for future action**

1. Ask your colleagues and/or supervisor(s) about how they make choices about which communities to publish for (e.g. research compared with applied publications and publications in the local language(s) compared with other languages).

2. Consider some specific journals which you have found most useful for your work, the languages used in these publications and the audiences they appear to be addressing. Given the value of these publications to your work, do they seem like appropriate or desirable outlets for your writings?

3. Consider whether there are particular scholarly communities you want to address now – or in the next five years – and whether there are other communities you would like to address.

1.7 **Useful resources**

- Nygaard, L. (2008) *Writing for Scholars: A Practical Guide to Making Sense and Being Heard*. Oslo: Universitetsforlaget/Copenhagen Business School Press/Liber. Chapter 4, 'Who are you talking to? Defining your audience', discusses a range of audiences in relation to the content of scholars' work and the types of knowledge different audiences might have.

- Murray, R. (2009) *Writing for Academic Journals* (2nd edn). Berkshire, UK: McGraw Hill/Open University Press. Chapter 1, 'Why write for academic journals?', asks you to consider their reasons for academic writing and publishing as well as the internal and external forces driving your interest in publishing.

- The 'Patter' Blog includes a wide range of resources and postings about academic writing and publishing: http://patthomson.wordpress.com/.

- Purdue University's Online Writing Lab offers a broad range of resources on academic writing, including a blog on grammar: http://owl.english.purdue.edu/owl/.

1.8 **Related research**

- Buckingham, L. (2008) Development of English academic writing competence by Turkish scholars. *International Journal of Doctoral Studies* 3, 1-18. This article documents the perceptions of 13 Turkish humanities scholars about their development of English-medium writing expertise.

- Swales, J. (1990) *Genre Analysis: English in Academic and Research Settings*. New York: Cambridge University Press. Chapter 9 of this seminal work provides case studies of multilingual scholars from Egypt, China and Iran writing for publication in English.

Information Box 1: 'International' publications

Whether a journal is considered 'international' is a complex and often subjective question. Some criteria that are used to determine whether a journal counts as 'international' can be the **language(s)** in which abstracts and articles are written; whether a journal's authors, editors, editorial board members and reviewers come from a **range of geographical and institutional locations;** whether the journal is included in **prestigious journal indexes;** and whether a journal has an **impact factor** and what this might be. However, especially outside of the Anglophone 'centre' (see Introduction), the term 'international' may act as a stand in for 'English', whether or not a journal represents other aspects of geographic and linguistic diversity. Similarly, in some institutional evaluation criteria, the term 'foreign' implicitly refers to publications in English, whereas in other criteria it may refer to publications in any language originating outside the local or national context.

Note

1   We use the American terms for academic ranks (assistant professor, associate professor and professor, which roughly correspond to the British system's terminology of lecturer, senior lecturer and professor).

Chapter 2

Making sense of institutional evaluation criteria

2.1 Chapter focus

Official institutional evaluation criteria play a key role for scholars in being hired, promoted, tenured and awarded grants as well as participating in other academic activities such as supervising doctoral students. Publishing activity is often a central focus of institutional evaluation criteria for academics. Although specific evaluation criteria are not explicitly articulated in all contexts, such criteria can exert powerful pressure on scholars' decisions about how to spend their limited time and other resources. Exploring the governmental or institutional evaluation criteria used in your context can help you decide how to navigate evaluation and reward systems in relation to your personal interests and commitments. In this chapter we present criteria from two contexts to begin this exploration.

2.2 Finding out about explicit and implicit criteria for evaluating scholarly publications

Data Example 2.1 includes some of the information that scholars must provide about their publishing activity as required by the public university system in Spain. Part A lists the documents that scholars are required to submit; Part B shows the range of points that each type of document can accrue. Look at these examples and consider these questions: How many points are awarded for different types of publications or scholarly activities? Do points vary with the language of publication?

Data Example 2.1: Documentation on publishing required when applying for an academic position

Part A. Documentation [to be submitted with application] [. . .]

4.2.3 On academic/scientific production and dissemination:

4.2.3.1 Publications

A) Articles in academic journals

For journals with an impact factor:

- The pages of the journal that include the title of the research, author's name, number and date of the publication of the journal, and the ISSN [International Standard Serials Number]
- The ranking of the journal in the impact index of the year the article was published

For journals without an impact factor:

- The pages of the journal that include the title of the research, author's name, number and date of the publication of the journal, and the ISSN
- The journal's system for selecting articles, the relative diversity of the members of its editorial board, its inclusion in international databases, frequency of its publication, place and date of the founding of the journal, whether it includes abstracts and key words

B) Entire books or book chapters:

Book title, author(s), publishing house, year of publication, ISBN [International Standard Book Number] […] and number of pages.

The book's index

For teaching books, the program of the applicant

For research books, the pages that describe the methodology and objectives of the project

For book chapters, the title of the chapter, its authors, number of pages […]

The system used by the editor/publisher for selecting chapters, the importance of the publishing house, how international the book is, the diversity of the members of its editorial board, inclusion in international databases, place and date of publication of the book, whether it includes abstracts and key words

C) Conference proceedings and public addresses [...]	
Part B. Research: Up to 15 points total	
Doctoral dissertation/thesis	Up to 6 points
Master's thesis, examination, or research project	Up to 1 point
European doctoral dissertation/thesis	Up to 2 points
Published books/educational materials	Up to 5 points each
Translations of own books into other languages	Up to 0.5 points each
Articles, book chapters, or conference proceedings	Up to 2 points each
Reviews	Up to 0.1 point each
Published addresses	Up to 0.5 points each
Funded research projects	Principal investigator: up to 2 points each Other team members: up to 1 point each
Conference presentations (not published)	Up to 1 point each
Unpublished addresses	Up to .025 points each

Translation of classic works with critical commentary	Up to 3 points each
Other translations	Up to 1.5 each
Technical reports to institutions	Up to 2 points each

(Spanish original; Agency for Quality, Accreditation and Forecasting of the Universities of Madrid)[1]

Comment

As indicated by the list of criteria, particular kinds of publications are clearly valued by the reward system in this context. For the most part, the items on the list are not unexpected although some of them may come as a surprise for some readers; for example, the points awarded for translated works or points awarded for a particular kinds of thesis – the European doctoral thesis. The ways in which publications are evaluated are explicitly set out here through the point system in Part B, where journal articles are awarded higher points than conference proceedings. However, implicit criteria are also at work, which we can see by looking at both Parts A and B. Notably, a key example is the distinction made in Part A between journals with and without 'impact factor' (see Information Box 3), which indicates that the status of a journal (as measured by impact factor) is one criterion used to evaluate the quality of articles that scholars publish. So while Part B does not seem to make this distinction – and in fact gives equal weight to journal articles of all types and to chapters, books and conference proceedings – we can see that other, more implicit criteria come into play, most obviously that an article published in a journal with an impact factor is evaluated more highly than an article in a journal without an impact factor. Another important implicit criterion relates to the language of publication. In this evaluation document language is not mentioned, the implication being that the criteria – as in the points – are used regardless of language. Yet we know from scholars' accounts that in practice different values may be unofficially awarded to articles published in particular languages as compared with other languages: English-medium publications are usually valued more highly than publications in other languages.

Data Example 2.2 shows some of the documentation that one scholar used for promotion ('reclassification') in another context, Slovakia. Look at the data and consider these questions: What similarities and differences do you see between the promotion report in Data Example 2.2 and the application requirements in Data Example 2.1? What assumptions appear to be at work in Data Example 2.2 about the value of publications in journals included in particular indexes and receiving citations?

Data Example 2.2: Promotion report by Martin, associate professor, psychology, Slovakia

An overview of selected quantitative data about the applicant, serving for his/her reclassification into the qualification grade IIa			
	Total	Since the latest reclassification	In the last five years
Number of own scientific works published in **foreign CC** [*Current Contents**] journals	3	2	2
Number of own scientific works published in **Slovak CC journals**	3	3	2
Number of own scientific works published in foreign journals other than CC and in proceedings	4	4	3
Number of own scientific works published in Slovak journals other than CC and in proceedings	30	30	12
Number of book monographs	2	2	2
Number of chapters in books	3	3	2

Table continued overleaf

Number of abstracts from **international** conferences	11	11	6
Number of SCI [Science Citation Index] citations	2	2	2
Number of citations other than SCI	6	6	4
Number of citations in diploma, candidate and doctoral works	14	14	14
Invited lectures **abroad** (number)	5	5	5
Participation in **foreign** scientific projects (number of times)	3	3	3
Leader of a scientific project (number of times)	2	2	2
Participation in scientific projects (number of times)	3	3	2
Teaching (number of credit hours per year)			Approx. 15/ year

(Slovak original, emphasis added. *Current Contents* is an index produced by the Thomson Reuters corporation.)

Comment

The application requirements in Data Example 2.1 and the promotion report in Data Example 2.2 share a number of characteristics. Both list a range of specific genres of publication, including various types of the key genre, journal articles, according to whether the journal meets certain criteria – being included in a particular index or having an impact factor. These criteria therefore implicitly value English in, for instance, in Data Example 2.1 the inclusion of the European doctoral thesis, which must be written in two languages, one of which is frequently English, and in Data Example 2.2, journals included in Current Contents. *The criteria differ in that while the Spanish criteria make a distinction between journals with and without an impact factor, the Slovak criteria focus on whether journals are included in particular indexes. As noted in Information Box 2, for journals to be included in certain indexes they must use English in some or all of their contents. In Data Example 2.3 the head of Martin's department in Slovakia explains how their evaluation system works.*

2.3 **One scholar's reflections on evaluation criteria**

Data Example 2.3 shows head of department Gejza's views on the evaluation system in his context. Look at his comments and consider the question: What do you learn about the ways in which evaluation criteria and practices have an impact on individual scholars' working lives?

Data Example 2.3: Views of Gejza, associate professor, psychology, Slovakia

'We have a minimum of what should be published in a year. If you do not meet these, then you are not allowed to get extra pay. You have a salary and you have a bonus and the bonus is flexible, but you must write certain types of publications in a year. We call these 'hard' publications; these are scientific journal publications and books, which are peer reviewed. All other activities don't count until they have these hard publications. This is our internal policy, which reflects the general policy of academia, so, for example, if you want to get an A grade in your evaluation, you must have journal publications, you must have citations, which you get from the journals, and you must have books, published. You fulfill the minimum of hard points if you have one or two papers in a non-*Current Contents* journal. If you have two papers in two journals which are not reviewed in *Current Contents,* this may also give you the minimum of hard points, and then you can add points from teaching and other activities.'

Comment

Gejza's comments signal the high value placed on publications in terms of whether scholars in his context receive a bonus at the end of the year, with certain types of publication considered as the minimum level of activity before other activities such as teaching are taken into account. As Martin's promotion report in Data Example 2.2 indicates, not all publications are considered as equal in this context – what Gejza calls 'hard' publications are those with the highest status – 'scientific journal publications and books, which are peer reviewed'. In the five years covered in Martin's report (Data Example 2.2), he has published two articles in 'foreign CC [Current Contents] journals', three articles in 'Slovak CC journals', and two books, all of which are considered 'hard' publications. In addition, Martin has published in 'foreign journals other than CC and in proceedings' and in 'Slovak journals other than CC and in proceedings'. As a result of this activity Martin's application for promotion was successful.

2.4 **Thinking about your practice**

1. What do you know about the evaluation criteria used in your context, particularly in relation to publications? How do explicit evaluation criteria affect your decisions about where to publish your work?

2. In most contexts both explicit and implicit evaluation criteria are used. Do you know about any implicit criteria used in your context alongside, or instead of, explicitly stated criteria?

3. How do both implicit and explicit criteria influence your decisions about writing for publication?

2.5 **Suggestions for future action**

1. Find out about the evaluation criteria used in your context in relation to publishing for different communities. How do these align with your own publishing interests and future goals?

2. Explore whether these criteria use terms such as 'international' or 'foreign'. Do they mention other languages? Seek your colleagues' or supervisors' understandings about the role of 'international' research and publishing activity in the evaluation system governing your work context.

2.6 **Useful resources**

- For a glimpse of journal publishing worldwide, if your institution subscribes to *Ulrich's Periodical Directory* (www.ulrichsweb.com), you can see its comprehensive listing of journals in categories such as academic/scholarly, consumer, corporate, government; and searchable by other criteria such as indexed, peer-reviewed, published in certain languages.

- Wikipedia.org includes a page, 'List of academic databases and search engines'.

- Belcher, W. (2009) *Writing Your Journal Article in 12 Weeks: A Guide to Academic Publishing Success*. Thousand Oaks, CA: Sage. Week 4 'Selecting a journal' includes the section, 'Evaluating academic journals', discussing how journals are ranked in indexes and notes that 'some scholarly associations also publish journal rankings' online (p. 119).

2.7 **Related research**

- Canagarajah, A.S. (2002) *A Geopolitics of Academic Writing*. Pittsburgh: University of Pittsburgh Press. This book focuses on issues of academic text production in the 'first' and 'third worlds' using illustrative material from Sri Lanka and the United States.

- Casanave, C.P. (1998) Transitions: the balancing act of bilingual academics. *Journal of Second Language Writing* 12 (1), 175-203. In this qualitative study Casanave explores the tensions and conflicts experienced by Western-educated Japanese scholars when they return to work in Japan.

Information Box 2: Journal and citation indexes

Journal indexes are searchable databases of specific journals and their contents (articles, book reviews, announcements, etc.). **Citation index databases** include references to articles and books that cite a published journal article or book. The U.S.-based company Thomson Reuters produces the dominant citation indexes as part of its ISI (Institute for Scientific Information) Web of Knowledge: these are the Science Citation Index, Social Science Citation Index and the Arts and Humanities Citation Index. In many contexts these indexes are seen as signals of rigor and quality for the journals they include. However, although they are widely known, these indexes list only about 24% of the approximately 98,715 academic journals published (Ulrichsweb.com, 12 April, 2013).

Two key criteria to be included in Thomson Reuters indexes are whether a journal is peer reviewed (see Information Box 14) (of the 98,715 academic journals listed above, 58,124 are peer reviewed) and whether all or part of the journal is published in English – which ranges from abstracts to entire articles. As a result these indexes exclude many journals published in other languages on linguistic grounds (among other criteria). A significant exception is the development of the Chinese Science Citation Database, which is the result of a partnership between the Chinese Academy of Sciences and Thomson Reuters. It is 'the first non-English product available within the Web of Knowledge' (http://wokinfo.com/products_tools/multi-disciplinary/cscd) and includes approximately 1200 scholarly publications.

Journal indexes/databases are also produced in other parts of the world and by a range of organisations. These indexes/databases include J-STAGE, produced by the Japan Science and Technology Agency; the Korean Citation Index (www.kci.go.kr); LATINDEX, 'a regional system of online information for scientific journals in Latin America, the Caribbean, Spain and Portugal' (www.latindex.org); DICE (Dissemination and Editorial Quality of Spanish Journals in the Humanities, Social Sciences and Law), funded by ANECA, Spain's National Agency for Quality Assessment and Accreditation (http://epuc.cchs.csic.es/faqs_en.html). In addition, in some contexts government bodies make lists of approved journals in which scholars should publish, such as that compiled by CONACyT (National Council of Science and Technology) in Mexico.

Note

1 We recognise that specific details of evaluation systems are changing all the time. The examples we include are used to illustrate common patterns.

Chapter 3

Responding to different institutional pressures to publish

3.1 **Chapter focus**

In addition to scholars' personal commitments and academic interests (as discussed in Chapter 1), their publishing agendas are influenced by strategic goals (as discussed in Chapter 2). Furthermore, institutional practices and rewards across contexts appear to be pushing scholars in several (sometimes contradictory) directions at the same time. Understanding how scholars respond to the demands of these evaluation systems can help you consider the implicit and explicit pressures in your own context and decide how to respond to these.

3.2 **The pressure to publish in English**

Data Example 3.1 presents two parts of the institutional criteria used to evaluate a Hungarian scholar's research and publishing activity as she applies for the academic doctorate (a degree beyond the PhD that is highly sought-after and prestigious). Read both parts of the institutional criteria and consider these questions: What aspects of scholarly publishing are highlighted in Part A? How might publishing be related to other listed criteria that do not explicitly mention publishing (such as criteria #5 and #6)? What more do you learn about the evaluation criteria from Part B?

Data Example 3.1: The academic doctorate, Hungarian Academy of Sciences

Part A: Criteria

1. As demonstrated by the applicant's publication history, having a well-defined research agenda in terms of scientific domain, scope, and methodology.

2. Maintaining active relationships with distinguished international scientists, significant professional groups and associations in terms of **joint publications**, professional cooperation, mutual visits, or participation in foreign institutions.

3. Having sufficient [. . .] original **scientific research** published in academic journals, research volumes, including studies published in a **foreign language**, as well as book chapters, and entire **research books** published in Hungarian or in a foreign language.

4. Receiving sufficient [. . .] **citations** referring to one's original research.

5. Having permanent research collaborators and students whose research agenda, methodology, and topics are largely influenced by collaboration with the professor.

6. Participating in the domestic scientific community through, for example, academic associations.

7. Having documented grant applications as demonstrated by research and development, international collaborations and publications.

(Hungarian original; emphasis in original.)

Part B: Evaluation Options

Note: Scholars are required to map their academic publishing activity against one of the two options.

Option A: [… to receive] a minimum of 200 PsychInfo or SCI citations and a minimum value of 8 on the h-index.‡

Option B: To accumulate a total of 120 points, as indicated here:

Monographs [books]	10 points*
Edited research volumes	6 points*
Book chapters	4 points*
Peer-reviewed article published in Hungarian or foreign language academic journals	4 points*
International conference proceedings	2 points*
	*Two extra points for foreign language publication

(Hungarian original; emphasis in original. †According to the Hungarian evalua-tion criteria included in Data Example 3.1, 'h-index = the number of those scientific publications whose number of independent citations are greater or equals to h. [For example, h = 10 means ten publications, where each publication has at least ten independent citations.] The h-index reflects data on the scholar's lifelong publica-tion activity.')

Comment

In terms of publishing activity, part A explicitly mentions co-authoring publica-tions, publishing in communities other than the local/national (e.g. 'studies pub-lished in a foreign language') and receiving citations to one's published work. The criteria listed in Part A which are implicitly related to publishing include having 'active relationships with distinguished international scientists', that is, connec-tions to academic research networks (see Chapter 12). At the same time, the criteria include exerting influence on others such as students and colleagues in the local/ national context. Part B, furthermore, clearly signals the importance of being cited by other writers, particularly in Anglophone-centre citation indexes (e.g. PsychInfo and SCI) and the importance of securing 'foreign language publications', which earns two points. However, official documents such as this may not explicitly dis-cuss all of the criteria being applied in a particular context. For example, the mean-ing of 'foreign' in 'foreign language publications' is not specified, yet increasingly the terms 'foreign' or 'international' are used in practice to mean 'English' (See Information Box 1).

3.3 **The pressure to publish in the local/national context**

Whilst the evaluation criteria above seem to place considerable emphasis on publishing outside the national context – through the emphasis on 'international' indexes such as Science Citation Index and 'foreign' publications – it is also the case that scholars may come under pressure to publish in the local/national language. This pressure may align with their personal interests but may also increase their already high overall workload, as is illustrated in the case of Julie in Data Example 3.2. Read the data and consider the questions: What pressures does Julie identify as leading her to increase her publishing in Hungarian? If she obtained the academic doctorate, in what activities would she and her departmental colleagues then be able to engage?

Data Example 3.2: Comments on the academic doctorate from Julie, associate professor, education, Hungary

> 'Earlier I didn't publish a lot in Hungarian but now I have to, because our department is very young and we need somebody who could pass this academic doctorate, and for that I had to be known locally and much more known outside. The requirement for university teachers to have this degree is new. You cannot start your department, cannot start an MA program if you don't have somebody who has this Academy of Sciences doctorate, you cannot sit on a PhD examination, you cannot be the head of an examination board, in a PhD comprehensive exam if you don't have this, and I'm the person [in my department] who is closest to this. I wouldn't be interested in it if my department didn't need somebody. The thing is, I have everything I need for this but everybody told me that I'm too young and I shouldn't try it now […]. The only way I can get it so young is if I have a good record of publications.'

Comment

In some contexts, degrees and other credentials beyond the PhD are required for academics to be able to perform certain institutional functions, such as evaluating PhD students, heading examination boards and launching academic programs. Obtaining such credentials may require scholars to establish both local and transnational reputations, as Julie's comments indicate in Data Example 3.2. When publishing is part of such criteria it adds pressure to publish that may or may not align with schol-ars' personal interests and commitments at a particular moment – in this case Julie feels a conflict in her publishing agenda between publishing for communities using English or Hungarian. In addition, Julie's comments about being told she may be too young to receive the academic doctorate signals additional implicit criteria at play – those related to contextual ideologies about who might be appropriate recipients of the academic doctorate. Data Example 3.3 shows Julie's publishing record, illus-trating the different communities in which she has published at different moments (in part in response to institutional pressures to get the academic doctorate). Look at the record and consider these questions: What patterns does Julie's publications record show in terms of her contributions to different communities? How do these contributions vary between 1996 and 2010?

Data Example 3.3: Julie's publications record across multiple communities

Community	Articles	Book chapters	Edited books	Books
1. National academic community in local/national/ state language(s)	1998 (3) 2001* 2004*			
2. National applied community in local national language	1997 2005* 2006 (2*) 2007 (3*) 2008*	2004 (2*)	2004*	
3. National academic community in medium of English	1996, 1998 (2) 2002, 2006			2000 2004 (2*) 2008*

Table continued overleaf

5. 'Intranational' academic community in medium of English	2003 2004*	2006*		
7. 'International' academic community in medium of English	1998, 1998* 1999 (3) 2000 (2) 2000* 2001* 2002* 2004 (3*) 2007* 2008 (6*)	2008 (2)* 2010*	2008*	2006

( ) = number of publications per year; *co-authored publication.

For types of communities see Chapter 1.

Comment

The trajectory of Julie's publications shows a shift from those written before finishing her PhD (from 1996 to 1999), which mainly appeared in national or regional journals in Hungarian and English (Communities 1 and 5), to articles published in English-medium 'international' journals (Community 7) after finishing her PhD. More recently, to bolster her qualifications for the academic doctorate, Julie focused on publishing for Hungarian-medium journals (Communities 2 and 3). As Julie's case illustrates, the publishing activity of scholars living in a complex academic world can shift according to changing personal priorities and commitments in interaction with institutional requirements and criteria.

3.4 Thinking about your practice

1. In terms of your current personal commitments and academic interests, how important is it for you to publish in a range of communities? Which communities seem to be important to publish in and for what reasons?

2. How might your publications activity play a role in your opportunities to engage in academic activities such as supervising students or launching research programs?

3. What pressures to publish in your context align or conflict with your personal commitments or priorities?

3.5 Suggestions for future action

1. Examine the evaluation criteria in your context, if available, and identify anything that seems unclear. Are pressures explicit and well-defined or vague? Talk to colleagues or supervisor(s) about their understandings of these criteria.

2. Discuss with colleagues or supervisor(s) whether their publishing priorities have changed during their academic careers. If so, have your colleagues changed how they respond to evaluation criteria and for what reasons? How do their experiences help you in contemplating your publishing priorities?

3. Find out whether there are any debates about evaluation criteria for research activity going on in your context and join in these debates.

3.6 Useful resources

- Swales, J. and Feak, C. (2011) *Navigating Academia: Writing Supporting Genres.* Ann Arbor: University of Michigan Press. This book introduces the kinds of career-related documents that scholars write besides publications, such as job applications, statements of purpose, cover letters to editors and recommendations for students.

- Paré, A. (2010) Slow the presses: Concerns about premature publication. In C. Aitchison, B. Kamler and A. Lee (eds) *Publishing Pedagogies for the Doctorate and Beyond* (pp. 30-46). London: Routledge. This chapter raises important issues for early career scholars to consider in making decisions about which communities to target and when.

3.7 **Related research**

• Li, Y.Y. and Flowerdew, J. (2009) International engagement versus local commitment: Hong Kong academics in the humanities and social sciences writing for publication. *Journal of English for Academic Purposes* 8 (4), 279-293. An exploration of how 15 scholars in Hong Kong respond to tensions between the growing pressure for publication in English and their desires to contribute to local knowledge dissemination.

• Petersen, M. and Shaw, P. (2002) Language and disciplinary differences in a biliterate context. *World Englishes* 21 (3), 357-374. This study documents variations in attitudes and demands for publication on scholars across departments even within one faculty, business administration, in Denmark.

Information Box 3: Impact factor

The push to quantify academic output and to rank the journals in which scholars publish has resulted in an increase in the use of a mechanism called the **impact factor**. A quantitative measure of how widely cited a particular publication has been (thus implicitly a measure of its influence within its field), the impact factor is defined as the ratio of the number of citations to a particular journal and the number of articles published in that journal in the preceding two years. Thus:

Citations to X journal in year Y (e.g. 2013)

Articles published in X journal in years Y-1 (2012) and Y-2 (2011)

For a journal to have an official impact factor it must be included in one of the ISI Web of Knowledge indexes, which provide data for the Thomson Reuters *Journal Citation Reports*. The majority of journals included in ISI indexes, and thus in *Journal Citation Reports*, publish at least some of their contents in English (for more information see Lillis & Curry, 2010: chap. 1). You can find a journal's impact factor at the ISI Web of Knowledge (if your institution has a subscription or owns CDs of citation reports published by the ISI) by searching the *Journal Citation Reports* for a particular journal. Some journals also list their impact factor on their website.

The impact factor has been criticized on many grounds: that it is a shallow measure of quality; that because the model originated with scientific journals it is less applicable in fields that disseminate knowledge more slowly, such as social sciences and humanities; that some research methodologies tend to generate more citations than others; that larger academic disciplines, in which more journals are published, have an advantage in generating citations over smaller disciplines; and that it is possible to influence the number of citations to a journal in various ways. In response to some of these criticisms Thomson Reuters now calculates a five-year impact factor to show the impact of a journal over a longer span of time, which is more useful for certain disciplines. Conversations are also taking place about other ways of evaluating the quality of research output, such as using the search engine Google Scholar to track citations (van Aalst, 2010). Notwithstanding these conversations and the changes made by Thomson Reuters, it is important to note that these discussions rarely address the question of whether citations are the best measure of an academic work's quality.

Chapter 4

Entering academic 'conversations' – finding out about scholarly conferences

4.1 Chapter focus

A key to success in publishing is becoming familiar with what Bazerman (1980) calls the 'conversations' that are taking place in your discipline: scholarly exchanges, debates and discussions about research topics, methodologies and theories. One way that scholars identify these 'conversations' is by attending local, regional and transnational academic conferences (also called meetings and congresses) to present research, learn about the work of others, meet colleagues and discuss shared interests with other scholars. Going to conferences can also be a way to participate in and build local and transnational academic research networks (see Chapter 12). Some conferences also offer information sessions with editors of key journals in the discipline as a way to help scholars understand the specific interests of various journals. In this chapter we explore some scholars' experiences with, and views on, attending conferences, to consider the value of conference participation to success in academic publishing.

4.2 Conversations and conferences

The conversations of academic disciplines can be identified in various communications about academic work, including public calls for conference proposals, articles or book chapters sent out to invite scholars to submit their work. Data Example 4.1 presents extracts from a call for conference proposals that Slovak scholars Martin and Gejza received. Read the call and consider these questions: What kinds of 'conversations' do you think will take place at the conference in relation to the theme of 'transitions' in post-communist areas? What kinds of conversations might take place in each of the conference topics listed?

Data Example 4.1: From a psychology conference call for abstracts/proposals

Call for Proposals

[Identities]* in Transition

International Social Science Conference, [location], [date]

During the last ten years there has been a growing interest in the so-called transition. Political, economic and sociocultural aspects of the post-communist transition have been analyzed from various social science perspectives. Nevertheless, one important dimension of this 'great transformation' in Central and East Europe is clearly missing: the study of [identities]. Due to the absence of studies on the new realities of [identities] (i.e. the changes caused by rapid economic and social transformation) we can only speculate on the emerging anti-[identities] overtones in current public discourse in the new democracies.

The [Identities] in Transition conference aims to fill this gap in the current knowledge and understanding of the effects of profound social changes that are still taking place in Central and East Europe. It will address an important question of whether [identities], aside from reflecting the new social reality, can also generate social tolerance and social capital necessary for a well-rooted democracy. A book consisting of the selected conference proceedings, to be published following the conference, will provide the first theoretical and empirical body of work that explores various aspects of [identities] in (post)transitional countries.

Organizing committee

[names omitted; scholars from Croatia, the United States, the Netherlands, Germany]

Conference topics [selected]

- Post-communist [identity] politics: Toward neotraditional moralities? (New political influences on [identities] in the post-communist societies between liberal democratic claims and neo-traditional practices ...)

- [Identity] research in transitional countries: Tradition and new winds
  (Methodological, as well a social and sociohistorical issues concerning area-related [identities] research)

- [Identities] and sex norms in transition
  (Transformation of identities in everyday life; increasing or decreasing equality ...)

- [Identity] representations in post-communist media

- [Identity and] minorities: New social movements

- Commercial aspects of [identity] in transitional countries

- Lessons from crosscultural research
  (Empirical studies that compare [identities] in transitional societies with the situation in other countries)

Format

The working schedule will be two sessions (morning and afternoon) per day for four days, with an additional day reserved for an excursion and the final round table discussion.

Deadlines

Abstract (up to 250 words) – November 1

Completed paper (sent electronically) – March 1

*As noted in the Introduction, to keep scholars' identities confidential, in data such as this we remove or replace information that might identify them and their research areas.

Comment

Conference topics are usually grouped into tracks, strands or sections that focus the interests of participants so they can submit proposals to the most appropriate section and during the conference attend presentations of interest. The list of conference topics provides a way to understand broadly some current 'conversations'. These conversations change over time as various issues move to the forefront of the concerns of the discipline. For the conference call presented in Data Example 4.1 conversations are likely to take place about politics, education, media representation, economics, minority populations and ways of researching these topics in relation to the focus of the conference.

4.3 **Submitting a proposal to a conference**

Data Example 4.2 shows extracts from the proposal that Martin successfully submitted in response to the call for proposals in Data Example 4.1. Read the proposal and consider these questions: Which conference topic/strand does Martin's abstract address? Do you think his abstract relates to conversations about a research topic, methodology, theory or a combination of these? Which words in the abstract link to these conversations?

Data Example 4.2: Extracts from a conference proposal submitted by Martin, associate professor, psychology, Slovakia

Comparative Qualitative Study of [Identities]* between the United Kingdom, Netherlands and Slovakia

Proposed section: Lessons from crosscultural research

Objectives: To explore differences and similarities in [identities] between United Kingdom (UK), Netherlands (NL) and Slovakia (SK), with a focus on identifying the background and precursors of [identities]. The study was based on the protocol for comparative qualitative studies on [identities]. The analyzed topics were: [A], [B], [C], [D], [E], [F].

Methods: In-depth interviews of the sample of 80 respondents in UK and NL and 30 respondents in SK aged 18 to 32 years with [identities] were made. After qualitative coding of the answers chi-square testing analysis was conducted. Compared are variables, where the observed distribution of frequencies differ significantly against expected distribution, and cells with significant adjusted residual value.

Results: (1) Pedagogical regime is most: repressive in SK, permissive in the NL, ambivalent and supportive in UK. [Identity] messages are most: moralistic in SK, manifold in NL and least frequent in UK. (2) Communication with friends about [identities] is most frequent in SK, and least frequent in UK. [...]

Conclusion: Fear and the holding of traditional values [...]

* Identifying information removed.

Comment

Under the 'Proposed Section' Martin indicates that he is sending his proposal to the conference strand called 'Lessons from crosscultural research', as his research consists of an international comparative study. His proposal specifies 'a focus on identifying the background and precursors of [identities]', thus identifying a historical focus to his research. At the same time Martin's proposal mentions 'a protocol for comparative qualitative studies', which suggests that he also wants to contribute to a conversation about research methodologies.

4.4 **Perspectives on attending conferences**

Scholars have a range of perspectives on the value of conferences and different experiences of attending conferences, as we explore in Data Example 4.3. Read the comments and consider these questions: From the reasons that Larya gives for attending conferences, what does she feel she gains?

Data Example 4.3: Reflections of Larya, assistant professor, psychology, Slovakia

'Slovakia is very small and when I chose the specific area of my interest there are very few people concerned with it, so I don't have proper feedback for the content of my work. So sometimes I feel like I am alone in the field. […] I knew about the first international conference in the Netherlands from a professor from Vienna, she is in contact with other people working in the psychology of [X] abroad. She gave me the information and I contacted the organizers. At the end of my presentation, I was very happy that discussion arose, which was stimulating, and I was given feedback in the session from people who are also concerned with the psychology of [X] and also qualitative research because this was my first qualitative research I had ever done myself. I was asked about my project and I was given some good ideas of what other variables to consider.'

Comment

Having found out about a relevant conference from a more senior scholar, Larya sought information about the possibility of attending the conference. Her experience of presenting in a larger and transitional forum was positive, providing the kind of detailed scholarly engagement with her research that she wanted to receive. As few local scholars work in her specialist area, Larya feels she has benefitted by meeting other scholars interested in similar topics, learning about their work and receiving feedback on her work.

4.5 Thinking about your practice

1. What conferences take place in your discipline in local, regional or transnational contexts? If you are unfamiliar with these conferences, who can you ask for information about them?

2. Have you submitted an abstract or proposal for any conferences in your local or other contexts? If so, how did you decide what to focus on for a conference, and for a particular strand, if relevant?

3. Has writing and presenting a poster or paper at a conference been helpful to you in preparing texts to submit to publication?

4.6 Suggestions for future action

1. Talk to your colleagues about which conferences they usually attend and what they find useful about specific conferences. Ask what strands of larger conferences they present in, what their experiences have been at conferences and how they have found funds to attend them.

2. Find a conference call for presentation/paper submissions on the Internet (by searching for 'topic + conferences' or looking at http://www. conferencealerts.com/). Note the submission deadline, length and format of the proposal/abstract, tracks/strands, useful information about the submission and review process and information about scholarships or travel grants.

3. Look at previous programs on the conference or association website to see what kinds of presentations were made. You may be able to find the presenter's email address in the program or on the Internet and send a request for a paper, poster, slides or handouts.

4.7 **Useful resources**

- Swales, J. and Feak, C. (2009) *Abstracts and the Writing of Abstracts.* Ann Arbor: University of Michigan Press, covers writing different types of abstracts, from conference abstracts/proposals to article abstracts. Task 22 presents useful questions for considering the practices of conference abstracts/proposals in your discipline.

- Nygaard, L. (2008) *Writing for Scholars: A Practical Guide to Making Sense and Being Heard.* Oslo: Universitetsforlaget/Copenhagen Business School Press/Liber, Chapter 9, 'Saying it out loud: Presenting your paper', gives advice on preparing a conference presentation, including visual aspects.

4.8 **Related Research**

- Langan, D. and Morton, M. (2009), Through the eyes of farmers' daughters: academics working on marginal land. *Women's Studies International Forum* 32, 395–405. In this article two female Canadian sociology professors analyze their experiences in academia, including reflecting on the role of conference presentations in research dissemination – and arguing for the importance of turning conference presentations into publications.

- Learmonth, M. and Humphreys, M. (2011) Autoethnography and academic identity: glimpsing business school doppelgängers. *Organization* 19 (1), 99-117. This reflexive (authoethnographic) paper explores the experiences of two British business professors attending academic conferences.

Information Box 4: Academic conferences and proceedings

Organization for a conference begins considerably in advance of the conference dates. Some conferences identify a particular theme related to current conversations or developments in the discipline or in society. Scholars may orient their proposals to this theme, although proposals on other topics may also be accepted. Common presentation formats include: keynote or plenary speeches by esteemed scholars in a discipline, symposia/colloquia (a set of presentations related to one topic or theme), roundtables (an informal discussion with other conference attendees), oral presentations (sometimes called 'papers', which may last from 10 to 30 minutes), poster presentations (where the presenter stands by a poster and answers questions from attendees), debates (a structured discussion or argument), teaching demonstrations, or workshops (in which presenters engage conference attendees in a discussion or activity).

The deadline to submit abstracts/proposals to the conference organizers can range from six months to a year – or more – in advance, so organizers have proposals (peer) reviewed and selected. Acceptance rates for conferences vary depending on their size, popularity, and policies – some conference organizers prefer to be as inclusive as possible, but others are more selective. Once proposals are reviewed, scholars are notified and in some cases given reviewers' scores and feedback on their proposals. Because conference proposals are due well in advance it is not uncommon for a scholar's actual presentation to vary from the proposal – if these are not major variations it's not necessary to highlight them or apologize for them. For some conferences scholars must submit full papers as the proposal or submit a proposal followed by the full version of the paper submitted before the conference takes place, limiting the possibility for changes to the presentation.

Some conference organizing committees also arrange the publication of proceedings from the conference. Proceedings are similar to edited books, which may be part of a series of books or a stand-alone edited volume produced by a publishing company or a scholarly association. In some cases conference papers may be submitted for inclusion in a special issue of a journal or be compiled on a compact disc or website. In other cases all conference participants are eligible to contribute papers to the proceedings; in yet other cases proceedings are invited and/or peer reviewed. The official value of conference proceedings in institutional reward criteria varies across contexts and disciplines; in addition, publishing a conference proceedings paper is typically considered 'first publication' of the work, thus other outlets such as high status journals may not consider it as a new submission (one not 'previously published').

Chapter 5

Identifying the conversations of academic journals

5.1 Chapter focus

What's of interest in the 'conversations' of specific disciplines differs across academic and geolinguistic communities and is reflected in the existence of a wide range of journals and their publishing formats (e.g. paper, online, paper and online, open access). Scholars must make decisions about where to try to publish, decisions that will be influenced by academic and personal interests. To make decisions scholars need to know which conversations are taking place in which journals. Initial questions scholars might ask include: which journals are concerned with my particular field (e.g. social psychology)? Is there a journal that focuses in particular on the methodology I prefer (e.g. experimental approaches)? Having identified possible target journals, you may consider questions such as: What theoretical or political positions are evident in these journals? Are these journals interested in publishing research from only particular regions of the world or do they evidence broad transnational interest? In this chapter we explore ways of becoming familiar with journals' interests to illustrate how you can identify which conversations you want to take part in.

5.2 Exploring journal websites

Journal websites are one place to become familiar with their aims, priorities and conversations. Data Example 5.1 provides information about two journals where Ernesto, a professor of psychology in Spain, has published. Read it and consider these questions: What is the main focus of these journals, according to their websites? How do they compare in terms of focusing on content, methodology and theory? Who publishes them?

Data Example 5.1: Two journals in the field of psychology

Psychological Review, American Psychological Association

Psychological Review publishes articles that make important theoretical contributions to any area of scientific psychology, including systematic evaluation of alternative theories. Papers mainly focused on surveys of the literature, problems of method and design, or reports of empirical findings are not appropriate.

Psychological Review also publishes, as Theoretical Notes, commentary that contributes to progress in a given subfield of scientific psychology. Such notes include, but are not limited to, discussions of previously published articles, comments that apply to a class of theoretical models in a given domain, critiques and discussions of alternative theoretical approaches, and meta-theoretical commentary on theory testing and related topics.

Consulting Editors: [see website for list of editorial board members]

Read Sample Articles

(http://www.apa.org/pubs/journals/rev/index.aspx)

Learning and Instruction, the Journal of the European Association for Research on Learning and Instruction (EARLI)

As an international, multi-disciplinary, peer-refereed journal, *Learning and Instruction* provides a platform for the publication of the most advanced scientific research in the areas of learning, development, instruction and teaching. The journal welcomes original empirical investigations. The papers may represent a variety of theoretical perspectives and different methodological approaches. They may refer to any age level, from infants to adults and to a diversity of learning and instructional settings, from laboratory experiments to field studies. The major criteria in the review and the selection process concern the significance of the contribution to the area of learning and instruction.

Extract continued overleaf

AUDIENCE

Educational psychologists, developmental psychologists, cognitive psychologists, educational researchers.

[Extracts from] Most cited articles published since 2008

Effects of studying sequences of process-oriented and product-oriented worked examples on troubleshooting transfer efficiency, Volume 18, Issue 3, June 2008, pages 211-222, van Gog, T., Paas, F., & van Merriënboer, J.J.G.

Motivations, perceptions, and aspirations concerning teaching as a career for different types of beginning teachers, Volume 18, Issue 5, October 2008, pages 408-428, Watt, H.M.G., & Richardson, P.W.

High-level co-regulation in collaborative learning: How does it emerge and how is it sustained?, Volume 19, Issue 2, April 2009, pages 128-143, Volet, S., Summers, M., & Thurman, J.

Attention guidance in learning from a complex animation: Seeing is understanding?, Volume 20, Issue 2, April 2010, pages 111-122, de Koning, B.B., Tabbers, H.K., Rikers, R.M.J.P., & Paas, F.

(http://www.elsevier.com/wps/find/journaldescription.cws_home/956/description)

Comment

*From these journal webpages it's possible to learn about their main focus and some similarities and differences. Most obviously, while they are both in the field of psychology, their areas of focus differ. **Psychological Review (PR)** articulates a focus on theoretical issues: as its webpage states, it 'publishes articles that make important theoretical contributions to any area of scientific psychology'. In contrast, **Learning and Instruction (L&I)** 'welcomes original empirical investigations'. It also specifies an audience of psychologists in the area of education, whereas **PR** does not specify an audience, perhaps because, as a high status journal in this field, its editors assume that readers such as Ernesto will know of its broad scope. **L&I**'s website provides links to articles that have garnered the highest number of citations (see Information Box 3). Both journals are published by scholarly associations: the American Psychological Association (APA) publishes **PR** and the European Association for Research on Learning and Instruction (EARLI) publishes **L&I** in conjunction with Elsevier, a commercial publisher. The websites therefore provide some information about the journals, but clearly do not provide all the information needed in order for* *a scholar to decide whether to submit an article. Ernesto regularly reads articles from both journals and in this way has learned about their key conversations and where different aspects of his research connect – for example, the more theoretical focus of* **PR** *compared with the more applied focus of* **L&I**.

5.3 **Working out the specific conversations of journals**

Whilst publishing in English-medium European or North American based journals – such as those indicated above – is often a goal for many scholars, a broader range of their commitments and interests also influences which journals, and which academic conversations, they wish to take part in. Data Example 5.2 shows information similar to that presented in Data Example 5.1, but highlights a journal published in Slovakia, with most of its issues published in the Slovak language but some published in English. Data Example 5.3 presents a case study of why one scholar, Danica, decided to publish in this journal. Read these examples and consider these questions: What do you notice about the location of the journal in relation to its goals? How might the location influence scholars' decisions about publishing in this journal? Why might this journal be of particular importance to Danica?

Data Example 5.2: Information about *Slovak Sociological Review*

SOCIOLÓGIA/SLOVAK SOCIOLOGICAL REVIEW is publishing original and anonymously reviewed papers written by sociologists in Slovakia and abroad. It brings information about sociological publication, activities in social sciences, about international conferences and sociological congresses.

It pays special interest to the problems of the civic society, to local communities, sociological problems of enterprises and work, problems of family, youth, social stratification and pathological phenomena. Papers from the history of sociology, sociological theory and methodology, findings of sociological research and public opinion surveys are published too.

The journal is not only for sociologists, but also for the broader public; university and middle-level school students, teachers, cultural, educational and social workers, activists of political parties and civic associations; for all who want to know more about our society.

The journal SOCIOLÓGIA is published six times per year; four issues in Slovak (with abstracts in English) and two issues in English (Slovak Sociological Review).

The journal is indexed in Current Contents: Social & Behavioral Sciences (Thomson Institute for Scientific Information) and other databases.

(http://sociologia.sav.sk/en/static.php?id=1153#a2)

Data Example 5.3: One scholar's publishing decisions

Danica is a young Slovakia-based scholar who has been researching issues of mobility and identity in Central Europe. She has been involved in several national and internationally funded research projects as a junior member of a team, is highly motivated about her research and committed to making it available in all relevant academic outlets. She is keen to make her and colleagues' findings available in international fora as well as in the specific region where her research is taking place and to emphasise the relevance of their findings to broader social debate and policy making. Danica has been invited, through local contacts, to submit a paper to *Sociológia* on several occasions.

Comment

The disciplinary field clearly indicated on the journal's site is sociology and its particular domain of interest is 'civic society'. However, in contrast to the journals in Data Example 5.2, the location of the journal is signaled as significant – referring to papers written by sociologists in 'Slovakia and abroad'. Thus whilst the journal does not state that it is interested in submissions only from Slovak sociologists – its reference to 'abroad' clearly signals transnational interest – by mentioning 'sociologists in Slovakia', it indicates that it welcomes contributions from sociologists in this region of the world. With regard to audience, the journal indicates that it is interested in involving (as writers and readers?) people from beyond academia, such as social workers and teachers, and by publishing two of its six issues a year in English, that it is interested in readers from both Slovakia and other national contexts. The high status of the journal is explicitly signaled through reference to being indexed by the Institute for Scientific Information (ISI), indicating its national and international status. From Danica's point of view the multiple-facing nature of this journal is particularly appealing. Publishing in the English-medium issues of this journal enables her to meet some of her transnational communication goals – to inform academics about her and colleagues' work – and at the same time, because the journal is likely to have a high profile in the region, indirectly to reach local policymakers. Being invited to submit a paper – as in this case through local scholars and networks (see Chapter 12) – does not guarantee publication, but is clearly a good opportunity, which Danica decides to take up.

5.4 **Thinking about your practice**

1. What problems, topics, research questions and methodologies are of most interest and importance to you?

2. What journals have you identified that consider the topics, theories and methodologies you are interested in? To what extent does/do the language(s) used by journals influence your interest in them?

3. What aspects of the conversations in these journals relate to your interests?

5.5 **Suggestions for future action**

1. Ask colleagues or a supervisor which journals and other resources they read regularly and how they become aware of the conversations of the discipline.

2. Some journal websites provide links to selected articles available for free. Reading them can give you a sense of the issues, problems and conversations the journal addresses.

3. It's also useful to skim read an entire recent volume (a year of issues) or more of a journal to see whether (and how) articles relate to each other by comparing topics, methods, theories, keywords, titles, abstracts and references.

4. Find out whether there are interesting and/or highly regarded journals that focus on particular regions of the world related to your interests.

5.6 **Useful resources**

- **Email alerts – journal tables of contents.** Some publishers offer email alerts – you can sign up on the journal website to get a free, regular email of the table of contents of each issue as it is published. If your institution subscribes to the journal, this email alert may be directly linked to your library so you can access the article directly.

- **Academia.edu** and **ResearchGate.net** are free websites where academics share research, receive analytics related to who looks at their publications and follow the work of other academics. You can search for scholars' work, sign up to receive alerts on papers published in various areas and create your own webpage.

- **Mendeley.com,** according to its description, 'is a free **reference manager** and **academic social network** that can help you organize your research, collaborate with others online, and discover the latest research'. Here you can organize citations and articles, join networks on particular areas and keep track of other scholars.[6]

- **Google Scholar** (www.scholar.google.com) is a website where you can look for scholars' articles by searching their name or topic keywords. It also provides links to citations to certain publications and, in some cases, links to full text articles or conference papers.

- **JSTOR access to articles:** The JSTOR database (http://about.jstor.org/individuals) aims to provide greater access to individual scholars by offering free access to 'early journal content' from 200+ journals, its free 'Register & Read Beta' account; 50+ public libraries in North America and a smaller number in other countries, including remote access; 'online access for alumni of some universities and colleges'; an 'Individual Access Program' to some publishers.

5.7 **Related research**

- Flowerdew, J. (2001) Attitudes of journal editors to nonnative speaker contributions. *TESOL Quarterly* 35 (1), 121-150. In this interview based study editors of applied linguistics and language teaching journals argued a key issue facing multilingual scholars as 'parochialism', that 'writers failed to indicate how their research addressed current issues in the international community of scholarship' (p. 135).

- Jaroongkhongdach, W., Watson Todd, R., Keyuravong, S. and Hall, D. (2012) Differences in quality between Thai and international research articles in ELT. *Journal of English for Academic Purposes* 11, 194-209. This article explores reasons for the under-representation of Thai scholars in global journal article output.

Information Box 5: Types of journal publishers and journals

Academic journals are published by a range of organizations that include university presses and departments, scholarly associations and commercial publishers. University presses have traditionally been a non-profit part of a university dedicated to publishing academic books and journals, often specializing in certain subjects. Many journals continue to publish via university or locally based publishers. At some institutions, departments or schools/colleges launch a journal and sponsor it, or it may be acquired by a commercial publisher. Scholarly associations, such as the APA and EARLI (discussed in this chapter), often publish well-known research journals as well as related applied journals and newsletters. Increasingly, because of economic constraints, university presses and scholarly associations are working with commercial publishers, such as Elsevier for the journal *Learning & Instruction*, which help them manage both submissions and subscriptions. But because these publishers operate for profit, this relationship may affect the association's publishing agenda. Journal editorial boards can face difficult decisions about which publishers to work with, trying to balance the potential advantages of being with a large commercial publisher, such as increased visibility of the journal, against the potential loss of independent control.

As mentioned in the Introduction online publishing is having fast-paced effects on the practices of scholarly publishing. Some commercial publishers (e.g. Sage) are publishing journals in a continual fashion, meaning that as each article is accepted and produced it is published separately from a traditional journal issue. Some publishers and journals are allowing authors to choose whether their articles are published with open access. In addition, as noted, open access publishing has spawned the rise of 'predatory' publishers aiming to profit by scholars' interests in seeing their work published (Beall, 2013). The various issues connected with on-line/open access publishing are potentially confusing and worth tracking.

Ulrichsweb.com is one of the largest directories of journals published worldwide (calling itself 'the global source for periodicals'), although it is not truly comprehensive. Types of publications included in *Ulrich's Directory* are:

Abstract/index*

Data base

Journal*

Magazine

Bulletin

Catalogue

Directory

Monographic series* (series of book-length publications, often by one author)

Newsletter

Newspaper

Proceedings*

Yearbook*

Report*

Handbook/manual* (edited books on a particular topic that aim to give an authoritative perspective on the topic; chapters are often contributed by experts in a field)

(*types of publications frequently recognized as scholarly, depending on the context, as discussed in chapters 1 and 2)

Ulrich's further distinguishes the 'content type' of periodicals as:

Academic/scholarly

Bibliography

Consumer

Trade

Corporate

Government

Other criteria that Ulrich's and others use for distinguishing journals include whether a journal is:

Peer reviewed

Open access

Available online

Abstracted or indexed

Included in *Journal Citation Reports*

Note

6 As an interesting example of how publishing companies are interested in benefitting from what begin as open access and free programs, Mendeley was acquired by the company Elsevier in April 2013, so in the future Mendeley may function in different ways.

Chapter 6

Joining academic conversations in a competitive marketplace

6.1 **Chapter focus**

A primary way that scholars go about getting their work published is by submitting an unsolicited manuscript to a journal. Identifying target journals and the conversations taking place in them can help you decide where to submit different types of work and consider how to tailor your texts for particular communities (as discussed in Chapter 1). However, getting published is a highly competitive activity, particularly when trying to publish in journals considered to be of high status, for example, because of their impact factor or other institutional criteria. The pressure on scholars to publish in journals considered higher status presents a number of challenges, not least that rejection is more common than acceptance and that scholars often go through the submission process with multiple journals in turn before publishing an article. As the road to publication can be a frustrating experience it can be useful to have several target journals in mind for a particular paper. Here we consider information on the status of journals and examples of scholars' decisions about identifying journals to target.

6.2 **Facts and figures about two journals**

Data Example 6.1 compares information about the two psychology journals introduced in Chapter 5. Examine this table and consider these questions: What do you notice about their impact factors and the geographic locations of the editors of these two journals? What difference might it make to rankings and impact factors that one journal has no limit on article length, while the other generally restricts articles to 8000 words?

Data Example 6.1: Information from two journal websites (2013)

Journal	*Psychological Review*	*Learning & Instruction*
Impact factor	7.784	2.768 5-year impact factor: 3.732
Manuscript length	There is no upper bound on the length of *Psychological Review* articles. However, authors who submit papers with texts longer than 25,000 words will be asked to justify the need for their length.	Manuscripts should be between 4500 and 8000 words in length (including references, tables and figures). Only manuscripts with multiple studies can go beyond this length.
Editor	**Editor** John R. Anderson [no affiliation given]	**Editor-in-Chief** Lucia Mason, University of Padova, Italy

Table continued overleaf

Other Editors	Associate Editors	Editors
	Jerome R. Busemeyer Indiana University Bloomington, USA	Sanna Järvelä, University of Oulu, Finland
	Charles S. Carver University of Miami, USA	Alexander Renkl, University of Freiburg, Germany
	Susan T. Fiske Princeton University, USA	P. Karen Murphy, Pennsylvania State University, USA
	Zhong-Lin Lu University of Southern California, USA	Jean-Francois Rouet, Poitiers University, France
	John T. Wixted University of California, San Diego, USA	Jeroen van Merriënboer, University of Maastricht, Netherlands
		International Editorial Advisory Board [see website]

Comment

*As Data Example 6.1 shows, the impact factor of **Psychological Review** (PR) is much higher than that of **Learning and Instruction** (L&I), possibly because PR covers a broader range of topics than does L&I. Moreover, the greater focus on theory in PR may also mean that its articles garner more citations (as theoretical articles may be read more widely than empirical work), as might the much longer article length (up to 25,000 words) compared to those published in L&I. In terms of location, the composition of the two journals' editorial boards is quite different: while the editor and associate editors of PR work at U.S. universities, the editor and many editorial board members of L&I are at European institutions. In fact, the L&I website characterises the journal as an 'international' journal. The location of editors is considered one factor in how 'international' a scholarly journal might be (Wormell, 1998).*

6.3 **Identifying target journals by rankings and citations**

How journals are ranked in particular indexes and the number of citations they receive (contributing to their impact factor, discussed in Information Box 3) are among the criteria that some scholars use to select target journals. Data Example 6.2 presents some scholars' considerations when choosing target journals. Read their comments and consider these questions: What do these scholars view as being important in identifying suitable target journals for their work? How do their perspectives compare?

Data Example 6.2: Scholars' views on identifying journals

Julie, associate professor, psychology, Hungary

'I would normally look on the Internet at the articles published in the last two years in the journal, at least the title and the author, and the abstract, and see whether my paper fits the journal. I also look at the editorial board to see if I know these people, what kind of work they are doing.'

Ernesto, professor, psychology, Spain

'When you read something by relevant people in your specialty, you can access where they are publishing. Anybody can tell you, well, these are the five most important publications in my field and probably the coincidence among different people would be great. There is also the Social Sciences Citation Index, which gives a clear reference about that. If you publish in a journal that nobody knows you have to justify for [institutional] evaluation the quality of your paper, so it's more economic just to try to publish in a good journal.'

Comment

Julie's comments suggest that the main way she identifies target journals is to investigate the range of articles published in recent volumes of journals to see whether her paper might contribute to a particular conversation. She also aims to get a sense of the editors and editorial board, as these are the people who would be likely to review an article she submits, to see whether she is familiar with their publications and areas of research. While Ernesto seems to suggest that it is relatively easy to identify the most prestigious journals in a field, it is important to note that he is speaking as an experienced scholar who has come to know this information over time and, as he indicates, by doing a number of things such as: paying attention to the journals where scholars in his specialist area publish; canvassing the opinions of other scholars about journals; and finding out whether journals are included in certain indexes.

6.4 **Responding to external pressure to publish in certain journals**

As Ernesto's comments signal, institutional evaluation criteria also influence scholars' choices of target journals or the decision about which journal a scholar might submit an article to first. Data Example 6.3 provides extracts from a 'text history' (see Introduction) – of one scholar's experience submitting an article to multiple journals in turn. Read the text history and consider this question: What role did the target journal's impact factor play in this scholar's decisions about which journal to prioritize for submitting this article [Journal A or B]?

Data Example 6.3: Text history of an article submitted to two journals by Julie, associate professor, education, Hungary

'I sent the article first to [Journal A] and the editor said it didn't have high enough quality because it just used one measure of [X]. She didn't seem to read the paper, though, because this test has several subcomponents. Actually the novelty was using all these subcomponents and she didn't even send it to reviewers. So I didn't change anything but the next day I sent it to [Journal B], my second choice. I was kind of hesitating between these two journals. But because the impact factor has been introduced, even in social sciences, when I report to my institution on research I have published, I have to indicate what impact factor the journal has. Journal A does have an impact factor but many of the journals don't have one, such as Journal B. So I thought I'd try Journal A first.'

Comment

Although Julie had initially been 'hesitating' about where to submit her paper, she decided to send it to Journal A because the journal has an impact factor, something valued by her institutional evaluation system. As she notes, her paper was not sent out for peer review because the editor challenged the quality of the methodology she used, and instead rejected the paper immediately. Whilst Julie was frustrated – she mentions that she felt the paper had considerable originality, or 'novelty', and she felt that editor hadn't read the paper properly – the next day, without making revisions, she sent the paper to a second journal she had already identified and where it was eventually published. Julie was pleased with her publication in Journal B as in her opinion this journal was of the same quality as Journal A, although it does not have an impact factor.

6.5 Thinking about your practice

1. Are there specific journals you would like to publish in? What criteria are you using to select these journals?

2. How would you prioritize the journals that you have identified, especially in terms of submitting a particular article?

3. At this moment in your career, how important is it for you to publish in what your field or institution considers a 'high status' journal?

6.6 Suggestions for future action

1. Look in reference lists of the articles/journals that you read regularly to see which journals are publishing the articles you feel are central to your (sub)discipline.

2. Identify possible target journals by asking colleagues/supervisors for their opinions about suitable and interesting journals. Rank the journals you have identified in order of how closely related you believe your article's focus to be to each journal - in the event that your top choice does not accept your paper and you need to send it to another journal.

3. For the journal you have identified as a top choice, try to work out its status by looking at whether it is included in relevant ISI indexes and what its impact factor (IF) is, if any. Discuss with colleagues or a supervisor whether the IF is considered important in your context or, if not, what other criteria are used.

4. Talk with colleagues about whether they have published in open access journals and, if so, what their experiences were, as well as how these publications were evaluated and rewarded institutionally.

6.7 Useful resources

- Belcher, W. (2009) *Writing your Journal Article in 12 Weeks: A Guide to Academic Publishing Success.* Thousand Oaks, CA: Sage, includes a section 'Selecting a journal' (pp. 99-138) reviewing types of academic journals as well as what Belcher calls 'nonrecommended' and 'questionable publishing outlets' that diverge from the book's focus on academic journals.

- *Cabell's Directories of Publishing Opportunities* (www.cabells.com) covers the disciplines of education, psychology, nursing and health sciences, computer science, business and information technology.

- Beall (2013) regularly updates his list of 'predatory' open access publishers that can take advantage of scholars' interest in publishing by, for example, charging large fees. See http://scholarlyoa.com/ (accessed 11 August 2013).

- Try out the Target Journal Evaluation Matrix (Figure 6.1) we have created as a place to organise and record the information you find out about journals.

6.8 **Related research**

- Flowerdew, J. (2000) Discourse community, legitimate peripheral participation, and the nonnative-English-speaking scholar. *TESOL Quarterly* 34 (1), 127-50. This case study traces the publishing experiences of a scholar who returned to Hong Kong after his postgraduate studies in the United States.

- Okamura, A. (2006) Two types of strategies used by Japanese scientists, when writing research articles in English. *System* 34 (1), 68-79. An exploration of the difficulties and strategies for publishing by 13 successful Japanese scientists and engineers, highlighting that more established scholars view publishing as a way of interacting with their audience.

	Journal 1	Journal 2	Journal 3	Journal 4
Title of journal				
Sponsoring association, if any				
Publisher (if different from association)				
Target community				
Main subject matter addressed				
Research methods used				
Theoretical frameworks used				
Abstract included (and length)				
Peer reviewed				
Impact factor, if listed				
Reference/citation style				

Figure 6.1 Target Journal Evaluation Matrix

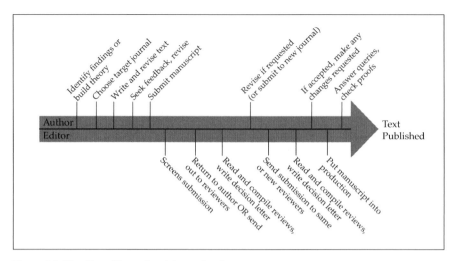

Figure 6.2 Timeline of journal article production

Information Box 6: Stages of journal publishing

An idealized view of the journal article submission process might look like the following, although in reality trajectories toward publication vary considerably:

- Author(s) identifies research findings/results.

- Author(s) chooses target journal.

- Author(s) writes manuscript, revises and asks colleagues and/or 'literacy brokers' for pre-submission feedback.

- Author submits manuscript. (In many contexts, it is generally not considered acceptable to submit the same article to multiple journals at a time; some journals will reject an article that is under review elsewhere at the same time and an author can be criticized quite sharply for this practice.) The manuscript is often submitted 'blinded', with identifying information about the author(s) removed for peer review. Increasingly journals accept manuscripts through electronic submissions systems.

- Editor screens manuscript to decide if its content and focus are appropriate for the journal. If not, the manuscript is returned to the author quickly without being externally reviewed.

- If the editor decides the manuscript is potentially suitable, it is reviewed by two or three reviewers who usually have between two weeks and two months to read the manuscript, recommend a decision and write a report. Recommendations range from: Accept, accept with minor revisions, accept with major revisions, revise and resubmit, reject.

- After reading the reviews the editor decides about the manuscript, which is communicated to the author along with reviewers' reports. If the author is asked to revise the manuscript, a deadline for submitting the revision may be given.

- The author revises the manuscript and resubmits (or decides not to). She may communicate with the editor about conflicting reviews or other issues.

- The editor may send the revised manuscript to the original reviewers or new reviewers or decide unilaterally about the revision, within weeks or months.

- After a manuscript is accepted the editor may ask the author for additional revisions by a particular deadline.

- The journal arranges for editing, typesetting, layout and proofreading of the article. Some journals use a copyeditor who sends queries and corrections to the author before typesetting. Some journals then use a proofreader to check for mistakes. The author will also be given proof copies of the article and asked to read for errors and return any corrections, usually within a few days.

- The accepted article may go into a queue or be published sooner if space is available or if the editor decides she wants to publish the paper quickly.

Chapter 7

Locating your work and forging conversations – whose work to cite and why?

7.1 **Chapter focus**

Acknowledging the work of other scholars is central to knowledge production and an important aspect of writing for publication. Citing others' work is a key way of demonstrating familiarity with relevant research and locating your work within existing scholarly conversations. Citations are also one of the key ways of shaping scholarly conversations, so there are important decisions to make about whose publications you want to cite in your work and why. In many writing guides the emphasis with regard to citations is often on making sure that the details are correct and formally presented following specific referencing conventions. Journals usually set out the conventions they expect to be followed as part of their submission guidelines (see Information Box 15). But, as the data examples below illustrate, in making and sharing knowledge globally there is much more to consider when thinking about whose work you are citing and why.

7.2 **Different ways of using citations in academic texts**

Here we show some of the ways citations are presented in academic publications: as 'non integral', 'integral' and as 'quotations'.[1] Read the examples and consider the question: What is the effect of different types of in-text citation on what gets foregrounded in the text?

Data Example 7.1: Types of in-text citation

Non integral: 'A recent longitudinal school study however evidenced that personal BJW strengthened teacher justice over time, and teacher justice increased the likelihood of good grades over the school year (Dalbert & Stoeber, 2006).'

Integral: 'For instance Cotton et al. (2002) found no interaction effect between work characteristics and student well-being.'

Quotation: 'Ouzoulias (2001) shares this point of view when he says that "in five-year old children a high degree of phonemic awareness reveals a greater level of development in terms of initial knowledge about written language" (p. 119).'

(Examples from Lillis, Hewings, Vladimirou and Curry, 2010)

Comment

Different ways of using citations have an effect on how you present ideas and the importance you attach to different scholars' work. Non-integral citations seem to foreground the idea or proposition. In contrast, integral citations and direct quotations seem to foreground the scholar who originated the ideas. Some writing guides (see 7.7 Useful resources) suggest varying the types of citations you use in your writing depending on whether you want to highlight an idea or a scholar who has introduced or discussed that idea.

7.3 Deciding who to cite and why

The most obvious reason for citing other scholars' work is that such work relates directly to yours: citations are a conventional way of demonstrating exactly how your work connects with that of others – for example, by adding, contrasting, qualifying and questioning. Citations are therefore a key way in which we build and grow areas of knowledge internationally. However, there is some evidence to indicate that the language in which academic writings are published affects how scholars use citations, which in turn may be influencing which knowledges are being circulated and where.

The table in Data Example 7.2 compares the citations used in two types of English-medium journal articles written by Portuguese scholars, by analyzing the works included in their final references lists. The two types of articles are: articles published in English-medium 'national' journals – that is, journals published in English in national contexts where English is not the everyday language of communication (e.g. an English-medium journal in Portugal) – and articles published in English in journals that are often classified as 'international' – these tend to be listed in the Social Science Citation Index (SSCI) and published in Anglophone-centre contexts such as the United States and the United Kingdom[2] (see Information Box 2). As you examine the table, what do you notice about the linguistic medium of the citations?

Data Example 7.2: Citations used in articles by Portuguese scholars in English-medium national (EMN) and English-medium international (EMI) journals (based on analysis of references in 34 articles)

	Citations in English			Citations in local/national language (Portuguese)	Citations in other languages	Total
	English total	*Translated into English*	*Non-centre English*			
EMN	439 (74.8%)	6	0	123 (21.0%)	25 (4.2%)	587
EMI	956 (95.3%)	9	0	34 (3.4%)	13 (1.3%)	1,003

Note: *English total* includes works written in English in the original work, which are the majority. *Translated into English* are works originally written in other languages and *Non-centre English* are works in English published in non-Anglophone centre contexts, for example, the *Asian Journal of Social Psychology*.

Adapted from Lillis *et al.* (2010).

Comment

Citations referring to English-medium publications are clearly dominant in the articles published by the Portuguese scholars in both the English-medium national (EMN) and English-medium international (EMI) journals. But it is also possible to see that this tendency is most marked in EMI journals, where a total of 95.3% of citations is to works published in English, in contrast with 3.4% of citations to texts published in Portuguese and 1.3% of citations to texts in other languages. These figures suggest that texts in English may be more likely to be cited than texts in other languages and that this tendency is greater in articles published in 'international', as compared with 'national', English-medium journals.

7.4 Scholars' perspectives on citation practices

Decisions about which works to cite are influenced by the particular area of knowledge scholars work within. These decisions are also shaped by many other factors, such as the language in which texts are available, the contexts in which journals are published and scholars' individual perspectives on citation practices. Read the comments below by three scholars. What differences and similarities do you notice about their perspectives?

Data Example 7.3: Scholars' comments on who gets cited

Margarida, associate professor, psychology, Portugal

'You can notice who is citing who and you can see that some lines of research try to ignore the other one which is really relevant. And now because citations and references are worthwhile, this is because citations count, I hate it. I hate it. And you say why are you not citing this, this and this? And they say because they prefer to cite these. In some journals you have to cut references. And you see that Germans cite Germans, people from Netherlands cite Netherlands, the Americans cite Americans. And I don't like this. This is not Science.'

(From Lillis & Curry, 2010, p. 139)

Ricardo, associate professor, psychology, Portugal

'I have always the concern to cite colleagues – the intention, so sometimes I try to find a way to cite a colleague.'

(From Lillis *et al.*, 2010, p. 130)

Ivan, professor, psychology, Slovakia

'Sometimes reviewers say you need to cut the number of final references. The expectation in English-medium ['international'] journals is that English writers should be cited. The pressure has significantly increased to produce English papers, which increases pressure towards citing English publications.'

(From Lillis *et al.*, 2010, p. 130)

Comment

These scholars' comments point to a number of issues they face: the desire to engage in academic knowledge exchange, which goes beyond national borders and where they believe issues of nationality should be irrelevant; the desire to publically acknowledge colleagues' work, particularly in a global context where the dominance of English means that scholars who research and publish in other languages are often ignored; the specific value of citations in academic work in terms of, for example, 'impact factor' (see Information Box 3) as indicated by Margarida – 'because citations count'; the way in which the convention of limited length of articles influences the critical decisions scholars face in terms of which citations to cut or include.

7.5 Thinking about your practice

1. Whose work do you want to cite in your writing and why? Are there texts or scholars you think it is more important to cite in writing for some communities than for others? (For communities, see Chapter 1.)

2. Are there scholars or work that you want to cite in your English-medium writings but think this may be problematic because a) the work is not available in English or b) reviewers may not value these citations?

3. What can you find out about your colleagues' citation practices? How do they make decisions about whom and how to cite?

7.6 Suggestions for future action

1. When you next draft a text for publication, look carefully at the ways you are referring to the work of other scholars by using the categories of 'non integral', 'integral' and 'quotation'. Consider whether the ways in which your text foregrounds scholars and their work is what you intend or whether you wish to change how you refer to certain scholars and their work.

2. Discuss with colleagues any challenges they face in referring to works published in languages other than English and how they deal with problems.

3. If you receive journal reviews that are critical of the way you have cited work published in languages other than English, discuss with colleagues how to respond. Some scholars, when they receive such comments, reiterate or emphasise the importance of such work in their paper.

7.7 Useful resources

- Feak, C. and Swales, J. (2011) *Creating Contexts: Writing Introductions Across Genres*. Ann Arbor: University of Michigan Press, pp. 59-78, covers the language used to discuss citations such as reporting verbs and active/passive voice.

- Giltrow, J. (2002) *Academic Writing: Writing and Reading in the Disciplines* (3rd edn). Peterborough, Canada: Broadview Press, includes a chapter on citations and their function in knowledge production.

- Nygaard, L. (2008) *Writing for Scholars: A Practical Guide to Making Sense and Being Heard.* Oslo: Universitetsforlaget/Copenhagen Business School, includes 'References: Giving credit where it is due', exploring referencing styles such as Harvard and Modern Language Association.

7.8 **Related research**

- Martinez, I.A. (2008) Building consensus in science: Resources for inter-textual dialog in biology research articles. *Journal of English for Academic Purposes* 7 (4), 268-276. This article explores the functions of citations in six biology research articles published in prestigious journals, tracing where they appear in the articles and what type of citations are used in which sections.

- Mansourizadeh, K. and Ahmad, U. (2011) Citation practices among non-native expert and novice scientific writers. *Journal of English for Academic Purposes* 10, 152-161. Reports on an interview based study that explores the citation practices of novice and expert Malaysian scholars, finding that more experienced scholars used citations strategically to support their claims while novice scholars used them to attribute knowledge to others.

Information Box 7: Scholars' experiences with academic publishing

In the past 15 years, a growing body of research has investigated how multilingual scholars around the world write for publication, particularly in English-medium journals (for overview, see Uzuner, 2008). A smaller body of work has begun to focus on the experiences of users of English as a first language and academic publishing (e.g. Carnell, MacDonald, McCallum and Scott, 2008). These studies fall into two broad groups: those empirically investigating scholars' experiences and perceptions and those presenting interviews with, or retrospective accounts by, scholars. Here we discuss the second group, as it can be encouraging and inspiring to learn about the challenges and successes that other scholars have experienced.

In *Writing for Scholarly Publication: behind the scenes in language education* (2003), Casanave and Vandrick collect 16 first-person essays about the growing importance of writing for publication to researchers and teachers in the field of language education as well as to post-graduate students en route to becoming professional academics. Many of the topics covered relate to chapters in this guide. About half of the contributors use English as an additional language; however, almost all contributors are working in Anglophone-centre contexts.

In *Writing Games: multicultural case studies of academic literacy practices in higher education* (2002), Casanave first interweaves autobiographical narratives of her experiences in academic writing with related theoretical discussions, followed by case studies of multilingual writers (including users of English as a first language). The focal scholars of the case studies include a bilingual doctoral student in the United States, novice researchers in Japan and established multilingual academics working in the United States. Through these case studies Casanave explores the metaphor of 'writing games', a notion grounded in social practice theories.

In *Reflections on Multiliterate Lives*, Belcher and Connor (2001) provide 18 autobiographical narratives (some in the form of interviews) written by established multilingual scholars from a variety of academic disciplines, linguistic and educational backgrounds from Austria, China, Taiwan, Finland, France, Ghana, Germany, India, Iran, Japan, Lebanon, Lithuania, Mexico, Sri Lanka, Puerto Rico and the United States. They share their struggles and success in mastering academic writing in order to shed light on its practices and processes.

Highlighting the experiences of postgraduates, in *Learning the Literacy Practices of Graduate school: insiders' reflections on academic enculturation* (2008) Casanave and Li work from the premise that entering postgraduate programs requires students to learn new literacy practices from those of their undergraduate programs. The book comprises three parts: 1. Learning to Participate, 2. Mentors and Mentees and 3. Situated Learning. Grounded in a social practice perspective, the book focuses on the social practices of graduate school rather than on textual features and text production processes. Its contributors include a range of scholars and students from a variety of locations and linguistic backgrounds.

Notes

1   These terms are taken from Swales (1990).

2   The distinction between 'national' and 'international' English-medium journals is more complex than outlined here. For discussion of the categories and the analysis of citations in these examples, see Lillis (2012), Lillis *et al.* (2010).

Chapter 8

Publishing articles or book chapters?

8.1 Chapter focus

As noted in the Introduction, academic journal articles and book chapters are genres that share similarities in terms of length, content and, in many cases, purpose and format. However, there can be important differences in the process of compiling edited books and the status of book chapters as compared with journal articles, so it is worth understanding the distinct practices of publishing chapters. Scholars can find opportunities for publishing chapters by responding to open calls, which are often circulated on Internet listservs (see Information Box 10). Direct invitations to contribute a book chapter may also come from a book editor who knows scholars or their work or through networks (Chapter 12). In this chapter we explore the potential benefits and drawbacks of writing book chapters as compared with articles, to help you think about where to direct your writing energies.

8.2 Responding to calls for contributions

Data Example 8.1 presents a call for book chapters circulated on the internet. After reading it, consider these questions: What are the timelines and procedures for selecting chapters for this book? What implications might these timelines and procedures have for a scholar's work schedule and publishing agenda? Why might this call be appealing to some scholars?

Data Example 8.1: Extracts from an online call for book chapters

Call for Book Chapter Proposals

Posted on May 5, 2011

Working title: Peace education evaluation: Learning from experience and exploring prospects

Editors:

Celina del Felice, CIDIN, Radboud University

Andria Wisler, Georgetown University

Proposals due: June 10, 2011

Notification of acceptance: July 1, 2011

Chapters due: November 20, 2011

Practice and research of peace education has grown in the recent years as shown by a steadily increasing number of publications, programs, events, and funding mechanisms. The oft-cited point of departure for the peace education community is the belief in education as a valuable tool for decreasing the use of violence in conflict and for building cultures of positive peace hallmarked by just and equitable structures. [Further description omitted.]

This volume has three inter-related objectives:

* […] to offer a critical reflection on theoretical and methodological issues regarding evaluation applied to peace education interventions and programming. …

* […] to investigate existing quantitative, qualitative, and mixed methods evaluation practices of peace educators in order to identify what needs related to evaluation persist among practitioners. …

* […] to propose ideas of evaluation, novel techniques for experimentation, and creative adaptation of tools from related fields, in order to offer pragmatic and philosophical substance to peace educators' 'next moves' and inspire the agenda for continued exploration and innovation.

Authors may come from variety of fields such as […] education, peace and conflict studies, educational evaluation, development studies, comparative education, economics, and psychology. Chapters may use any methodology and must not be previously published or under review for publication elsewhere. Proposals from practitioners, educators, and scholars at all career levels are welcome. Please

submit a 500-word proposal in English for a book chapter to the Managing Editor
[…].

The proposal should offer an abstract/overview of the chapter manuscript and
indicate to which objective of the book the chapter would contribute. Please
include five keywords, a proposed book chapter title, full name, email address,
institution (if applicable), and short biographical note of maximum 150 words
with your proposal.

All proposals will go through a review process. If your proposal is accepted, the
editors request your full manuscript of 5,000-7,000 words. […] Please conform to
the APA citation format for the proposal and accepted manuscript. This edited
volume is scheduled for publication in late Spring 2012 within the Peace Education
Series of Information Age Press. (http://freshscholarship.com/1503-call-for-book-
chapter-proposals)

Comment

*The proposed timeline for this edited book is short, with seven months between the
submission of the proposal and delivery of the 7000-word chapter manuscript. This
timeline implies that a scholar whose proposal would be accepted would have already
begun research and writing in order to meet the deadline. In other cases editors
might set a longer schedule so that contributors would have more time to prepare
submissions. Despite the short timeline in this call for chapters – which may present particular challenges if translation or other language work is to be involved (see
Chapter 11) – it might appeal to scholars who are not only working on the topic
'peace education' but are particularly interested in interdisciplinary research, given
the mention of a range of disciplines including economics and psychology.*

8.3 Responding to an invitation to write a book chapter

Data Example 8.2 presents a text history of a chapter that Diana, an education scholar, contributed to an edited book. This text history may help you
understand some of the practices and processes related to the preparation of
an edited book, as well as consider advantages and disadvantages of writing
a chapter. Read the text history and answer these questions: What motivated

Diana to turn her conference poster into a book chapter? Why did she decide to prepare a chapter for this particular book?

Data Example 8.2: From conference poster to book chapter

After giving a poster presentation at a conference in Vienna, Diana was invited by a Portuguese colleague to contribute a chapter to an English-medium book that the Portuguese colleague and a Finnish colleague were planning to co-edit. Diana reported her feelings about the invitation: 'When I was invited to be an author in that book, as I enjoyed very much the subject that I approached in the poster, I enlarged it and I made a proposal to publish it'. The Canadian husband of a friend helped Diana with the English in her text. After submitting the chapter, Diana received feedback from the Portuguese editor and a peer reviewer. Then the book was delayed when the Portuguese colleague became ill and the Finnish co-editor moved to United States. The book was finally published four years after the Vienna conference. Despite the delay, Diana was pleased to have her work published in the book, as she felt it represented 'a good set of articles and the people are very international, it's a very international book'.

Comment

Clearly, contributing a book chapter can offer an opportunity to collaborate on a publication on a specific topic. In addition, because edited books are often organized through academic research networks, as in this case, a chapter may have a better chance of being accepted than would an article submitted to a journal. In this respect, it's important to note that editors and reviewers of book chapters often have a different orientation towards the chapters they are reviewing than do journal reviewers; book editors are often more interested in finding ways to support and develop the text rather than simply to evaluate (and potentially reject) it. Book editors may also have access to resources such as collaborators who can give useful feedback. One potential practical disadvantage, as illustrated in Data Example 8.2 and as we consider below, is that schedules for the production of books are often less strict as compared with journals, so work may take longer to be published.

8.4 **Delays in a book's publication**

Data Example 8.3 shows a letter to contributors from one of the editors of the book in Diana's text history. Read the letter and consider this question: What drawbacks does the editor's letter suggest about choosing to contribute a chapter to an edited book?

Data Example 8.3: Editors' update letter

27 November 2007

Dear colleagues,

We all began writing a book on [X] in 2005 but then I got seriously ill, the other editor [name] went to the [United] States and she had too much work there, and some of you also sent chapters much later than expected. We also waited some months for an answer from another publisher that never answered us. Thus, we were only able to have the book contract with the publisher in October 2007.

Now that this is done and that we have almost all the chapters – [Author A] is joining us and sending his chapter soon – I am writing to you with a new timeline, that we must respect. As you know, when the contract is signed there are mandatory dates to deliver the manuscript. Please answer me and confirm that you received this email. We want to have you all in the book and the publishers were most positive in the feedback they sent, based on the abstracts and extended summaries we wrote.

Most of the papers are between 20 and 26 pages. We estimated an average of 25 pages for each paper, thus those who papers are this long are fine. I enclose the publisher's norms, so you can use them in the revised first draft you send me at the end of December. Until then, those who wrote their papers in 2005 or 2006 and wish to use more recent references, or slightly change any points, can do it. But please, do not completely change the papers.

[Authors B and C] wrote a short version of their chapter for the [X] 2005 symposium and they promised to send a longer version to this book. Thus, I do hope they will send a longer version. [Author D's] chapter is 61 pages long + tables and figures. Thus, it needs to be cut. All the other chapters can be as long as they are now. Thus, please, just read them again and see if you want to update any details/ points.

I enclose the new timeline according to the contract we signed with the publishers. I also enclose the Index of the book. Best regards and hope to hear from you soon!

Comment

As illustrated in Data Example 8.3, delays can be one drawback to publishing book chapters. These delays can be caused by the time for editors to obtain a contract with a publisher, which can require the proposal to be revised; late delivery of chapters by some contributors; and editors having heavy workloads or personal issues that delay the process. In terms of securing readership, other potential drawbacks can be the difficulty of finding published chapters of edited books through library databases. Chapters in edited collections are often less visible and less easily accessible than journal articles, so book chapters may not reach as many readers. This said, some databases such as ebrary, Ebook Library, Netlibrary and Google Books now index books by searching the full text and assigning them subject categories.

8.5 Thinking about your practice

1. In your discipline, do you find relevant research published in edited books as well as in journals? Does it seem that many scholars in your disciplinary specialism publish book chapters?

2. How are edited book chapters evaluated in your local rewards system (see Chapter 2)?

3. How relevant, important or useful do you think publishing a book chapter would be for you at the moment?

8.6 Suggestions for future action

1. Discuss with colleagues the value of edited book chapters in your context. Do your colleagues recommend that you write chapters in edited books as part of your publications?

2. Seek out the official evaluation criteria in your context to understand how book chapters are valued as compared with journal articles and other genres.

3. Consider why contributing to an edited book might be important. Could it be, for example, a way of collaborating with colleagues to develop a particular theoretical or methodological approach?

8.7 **Useful resources**

- Henson, K.T. (2005) *Writing for Publication: Road to Academic Advancement*, Boston, MA: Allyn & Bacon, Chapter 11, Planning for Success, includes a section about drawing on published articles to write book chapters that are later included in textbooks or professional handbooks.

8.8 **Related research**

- Edwards, L. (2012) Editing academic books in the humanities and social sciences: Maximizing impact for effort. *Journal of Scholarly Publishing* 44 (1), 61-74. This article advocates for the strengths of edited scholarly books and makes suggestions to those wishing to edit such volumes.

- Huang, M. and Chang, Y. (2008) Characteristics of research output in social sciences and humanities: From a research evaluation perspective. *Journal of the American Society for Information Science and Technology* 59 (11), 1819-1828. This article provides a survey of publishing output of scholars across disciplines in terms of journal articles, book chapters and books, noting considerable variation.

Information Box 8: Publishing a chapter in an edited collection

Compiling an edited book differs from journal publishing in key ways, particularly in the beginning stages and peer review. A scholar may want to propose an edited book to a publisher or may already have interest indicated or a contract in hand from a publisher. The editor may put out a call through listservs and other media to solicit abstracts, proposals or outlines for a chapter from the scholarly community at large. Alternatively, an editor may invite particular authors to submit a proposal which is reviewed by the editor(s) and possibly by peer reviewers. Some edited books are authoritative 'handbooks' on a disciplinary topic, which are considered reference books by librarians and scholars; these may be updated periodically. In some cases edited books are planned for publication to follow a conference or seminar (these may differ from 'proceedings' of a conference in being more selective or by not using the term 'Proceedings' in the title).

Some editors call for proposals and/or outlines to be submitted before the complete chapter manuscript is accepted, as in the examples in this chapter. After a chapter is submitted to a book editor it is usually reviewed by the editor(s) and may go through peer review – or it may be reviewed only by one or more editors. In some cases, to create a cohesive text, editors make chapter drafts available to other contributors so that they can draw on each other's chapters as they revise their own.

It is important to recognize that published book chapters carry varying value in different reward systems. Belcher (2009) includes book chapters in her list of 'Questionable publishing outlets' based on some of the points raised here: uneven peer review or other quality control mechanisms, potential for delay, and greater difficulty in accessing edited books than journals. She recommends edited books as being 'best reserved to reprint articles that have already been published in peer-reviewed journals [... or] articles that are unlikely to be accepted by peer-reviewed journals because they are too narrow or descriptive' (p. 106). However, scholars in many disciplinary areas often consider it important to publish new work in edited books.

Chapter 9

Understanding trajectories and time in the publishing process

9.1 **Chapter focus**

Writing a text for publication requires considerable time – many months can be needed for a writer or co-authors to produce multiple drafts before a paper is ready to be submitted to a journal or edited book. In fact, it can sometimes take years for an article to be published, depending on schol-ars' and collaborators' available time and other obligations and interests, as well as time needed in the submission, review and revision process. Time is required for getting funding and conducting research, locating and read-ing the relevant research literature, drafting and revising texts and respond-ing to feedback before and after submission. In some cases, scholars revise manuscripts and (re)submit them to a number of different target journals in sequence before getting published. In this chapter we examine the role of time in preparing and submitting texts for publication in order to help you plan for your academic writing.

9.2 **Time and writing**

Many scholars face challenges in finding time for the academic writing they want or need to do among their other responsibilities (teaching, supervis-ing students and administrative work), as Data Example 9.1 suggests. Read these scholars' comments and consider these questions: What tensions about the availability of time in their schedules do the scholars identify? How do they try to resolve these tensions?

Data Example 9.1: Finding time for research writing

Perspectives of Amalia, associate professor, psychology, Portugal

'Here we are always teaching or marking, you know, so we don't have any time. You have to organize your day and then you will find something. For me it was really difficult because sometimes you have new subjects to teach, for example, or you always have things to work on and when you are writing something you need time especially for that. When I said two months to write an article, I meant two months only with the article, so if I'm teaching then I will need four, five months. You always have to come back to the article, and think "Why did I write this?".'

Text history of Diana, associate professor, education, Portugal

Diana responded to a call for book chapters posted on a listserv in her disciplinary sub-specialism. The book editors accepted Diana's 600-word proposal for a theoretical chapter. However, because of her workload Diana did not feel she could write the 25 to 30 page chapter in English by the deadline: 'I started to work on the chapter, but then I had lots of work, so it was difficult.' After abandoning the project, Diana was disappointed: 'My feeling is that I lost an opportunity.' However, she later developed some of her ideas in a paper that she presented at a seminar with key scholars in her discipline.

Comment

Both Amalia and Diana emphasize the challenge of finding time to write in their busy academic lives. Amalia discusses the need to 'organize your day' to find time to write, while Diana indicates that even with the best intentions it can sometimes be impossible to fulfill writing commitments. However, as Diana also notes, despite disappointments about not completing papers, some work can be transformed into texts for other opportunities (in this case a seminar presentation) which can later become published articles or chapters. In regard to the case Diana discusses here, she later developed the ideas from her original chapter proposal into another paper. This example illustrates how scholars may subsequently develop work that did not come to fruition at a particular moment – that pursuing a research agenda over time provides multiple opportunities to disseminate research.

Data Example 9.2: Time needed for drafting

Writing a complex academic paper often takes considerable amounts of time, as scholars' comments here demonstrate. As you read, consider the challenges they face in producing articles. What issues do they raise about writing in a number of languages?

Ernesto, professor, psychology, Spain

'For me, writing is a very tough task. It is very, very difficult. In fact, I regularly write six, seven, eight, ten versions of the same paper, revise them, and in the end I decide to finish. […] Writing clearly, being precise and coherent, it's difficult either in English or in Spanish. […] To write a very good paper is a long, it's a tough job. It takes a long time.'

Diana, associate professor, education, Portugal

'Some of the issues I am writing about, they are difficult, so what is necessary is time to put ideas in good syntax and a good manner. I do lots of editing and I know that writing is a very complex activity, at least in order to publish. The problem that I have writing in English is the same that I have when I am writing in Portuguese, plus turning ideas around to put in the direct way of English grammar. Sometimes even in Portuguese to find out the correct syntax for an idea is not a simple task, so imagine doing that in English.'

Comment

Both scholars indicate a simple fact – but one easily forgotten – that producing academic papers involves considerable time and hard work, even for experienced scholars like them. They focus on aspects of academic knowledge production that require a lot of time. They also indicate that they write regularly in two languages and that expressing complex ideas is challenging in both languages. In the next section we explore the time span of one text history of a published article.

9.3 **The trajectory of one article toward publication**

In addition to the time involved in writing and revising a text for publication, time is needed to respond to feedback from co-authors, other colleagues and publishing gatekeepers both before and after submission of a text. Data Example 9.3 summarises the events involved in the trajectory of an article written by Carla, an associate professor of psychology from Spain, and a British colleague from a related discipline with whom she worked. During this time Carla's collaborator died suddenly, which of course had a major impact on the process. Read the text history and consider these questions: How much time elapsed at each moment in this trajectory, from writing to revising to resubmitting the article and repeating this cycle? In total? What key events influenced the trajectory of this text?

Data Example 9.3: Text history of a co-authored article

Time	Event in the publishing timeline
1999	Carla arranged to visit the United Kingdom for six weeks to conduct experiments in her colleague's laboratory.
2000	The British colleague presented their joint research results at a U.S. conference. Later the conference abstract was published.
2001	The British colleague drafted the article in English and sent it to Carla, who was second author, for her comments.
January 2002	Carla sent feedback on the article to her colleague.
May 2002	The British colleague died suddenly. Carla subsequently took over preparing the article for submission.
June 2002	Carla submitted the manuscript to *Journal A*, the top U.S. journal in her colleague's field, which he had identified as their first target journal.
August 2002	The editor of *Journal A* sent reviews to Carla, asking for 'major changes' in response to the reviews.

Table continued overleaf

March 2003	Carla resubmitted the article with a cover letter detailing changes made in response to reviews.
April 2003	*Journal A* editor asked Carla to make additional revisions.
June 2003	Carla revised and resubmitted the article.
August 2003	*Journal A* editor rejected the article because the reviewers did not agree on whether to recommend it for publication.
December 2003	Although disappointed, Carla chose a new target, an English-medium European journal, and submitted the article to *Journal B*.
April 2004	*Journal B* editor accepted the article pending minor revisions.
May 2004	Carla submitted the revised draft to *Journal B*.
2005	Article was published in *Journal B*.

Comment

In this text history some six years elapsed between initial submission of the article to Journal A and its ultimate publication in Journal B. Key events with regard to the processes of publication were Journal A's requests for major revisions, rejections and the identification of, and submission to, the second journal. The most significant event in relation to co-authoring – and a personal tragedy – was the death of Carla's collaborator, which meant that she had to take on sole responsibility for getting the article through the submission process. Nonetheless, the time span involved in this text history is not uncommon. During and after conducting research, time is required to write an article, receive feedback from co-authors and others and wait for gatekeepers' reviews and decisions. Delays can happen at any of these points and because of the demands of an author's other responsibilities – for example, Carla was at the time head of her department's graduate program and conducting other research. In addition, Carla's experience with making requested revisions for a journal and then later having the manuscript rejected is not rare, because reviewers and editors may not deem the revisions sufficient for publication.[1]

9.4 **Thinking about your practice**

1. How much time can you find in your schedule for writing and other tasks related to research? Does your job description specify a certain amount of time to be devoted to research?

2. What are your ideal conditions for writing? How can you write even when these conditions are not available?

3. Are there experienced scholars in your context who can advise you during the publishing trajectory – such as how to interpret editors' and reviewers' comments on your submissions (see chapters 14 and 15)?

9.5 **Suggestions for future action**

1. Talk to colleagues about their strategies for creating or protecting time in their schedules for writing and identifying ways that your institution supports this goal.

2. Consider how you can exchange giving feedback and support to other writers in order to improve each other's texts before submitting manuscripts or after receiving communications from gatekeepers.

9.6 **Useful resources**

- Belcher, W. (2009) *Writing Your Journal Article in 12 Weeks*. Thousand Oaks, CA: SAGE, has a chapter, 'Designing your plan for writing', in which she suggests developing a writing plan as a first step to creating time in your schedule and proposes the value of a regular writing practice and making writing a social activity by involving others.

- Murray, R. (2009) *Writing for Academic Journals* (2nd edn). Berkshire, UK: McGraw-Hill/Open University Press, addresses emotional barriers to writing, including 'procrastination, guilt, fear, and anxiety'.

- Nygaard, L. (2008) *Writing for Scholars: A Practical Guide to Making Sense and Being Heard*. Oslo: Universitetsforlaget/Copenhagen Business School

Press/Liber, Chapter 2, 'Getting started: developing good writing habits', proposes strategies like aiming to 'set aside time, make space, develop productive writing rituals [...] take advantage of deadline pressures'.

9.7 **Related research**

- Englander, K. (2009) Transformations of the identities of nonnative English-speaking scientists as a consequence of the social construction of revision. *Journal of Language, Identity, and Education*, 8, 35-53. This article investigates how Mexican scientists responded to gatekeepers' feedback on their texts and their revision practices, including the role of time.

- García Landa, L. (2006) Academic language barriers and language freedom. *Current Issues in Language Planning* 7 (1), 61-81. This study documents the time spent by Mexican scholars in their efforts to publish their research in English.

Information Box 9: Time in production after acceptance

After an article has been accepted by a journal (or an edited book), the manuscript is typeset and formatted according to the journal's style and the author will be sent 'proofs' to check. Both authors and journal or book editors are involved in reviewing proofs of a journal's articles. The production staff (copyeditors, proofreaders) may include queries to be answered; reviewers of proofs also check the quality of the typesetting and formatting. Typically authors are only given a few days to read proofs and send corrections to the production staff so the journal can meet its schedule. To this end staff may communicate with authors before the expected date to reserve time for proofs. Although journals and publishing houses usually have staff who 'proofread' (check for errors and format) a text, the author(s) has final responsibility to check the text's typesetting and layout for accuracy. To return proofs according to schedule, authors often need to shelve other work at short notice.

As an author, it can be challenging to proofread a text that you have worked on for a long time, as writers often see what we expect the text to say and sometimes do not see errors. Even after using a spell check program before submitting the manuscript, you may find mistakes such as typographical errors, homonyms (words that sound the same but are spelt differently) and other words that spell check may not catch. In addition, mistakes often show up in headings, subheadings, footnotes, text and numbers in figures and tables and their captions, including the sequence of the numbers for each figure and table and references. It is useful to ask a co-author, colleague or friend to read the proof aloud while you read along with a printout of your submitted manuscript (after any revisions were made). Look for whether the heading levels have been typeset in accordance with your intended structure (and following the journal's style). This step can help you notice if material has been dropped or moved during layout. Another way to catch errors is systematically to proofread your text multiple times, each time looking at the components of the article (headers, graphics, references, footnotes, etc.).

With the advent of online publishing, journals are increasingly often making the pre-print version of an article available online before it is officially published. This version has been laid out, proofread and approved for publication, but does not have the volume, issue or page numbers assigned. Rather than waiting for the journal issue to 'appear', online preprint publication now means that the article is available to be read and used. However, it cannot yet be cited as published without the specific citation information.

Note

1   See Lillis and Curry (2006a) for analysis of the reviewers' feedback on Carla's article and her responses.

Chapter 10

Accessing resources for writing for publication

10.1 **Chapter focus**

To support academic publishing, scholars draw on a range of material resources: from research funding (equipment, space, research assistance, course release time, etc.) to bibliographic resources and money for travel to collaborate on research and to attend conferences. These material resources also enable scholars to gain access to the intellectual and social resources such as research networks and literacy brokers, who support participation in publishing (see Chapters 12 to 14). In this chapter we explore the importance of such resources for publishing and some of the ways in which multilingual scholars locate such resources in their immediate contexts or elsewhere.

10.2 **Strategies for accessing bibliographic resources**

Although the internet has made some bibliographic resources more accessible than before, scholars in many contexts still lack access to key resources necessary for producing academic articles, not least because of the high cost of books and academic journal subscriptions. Data Example 10.1 illustrates resources that scholars need, yet have difficulty accessing. Read these examples and consider these questions: What are the resources that scholars need and how do they access them? How useful might their strategies be to other scholars?

Data Example 10.1: Accessing key resources

Larya, assistant professor, psychology, Slovakia

'I communicated with a professor in Vienna and she gave me her articles published in this journal. Also, if I find a citation to literature I can find the author's address on the Internet and ask him to send me a reprint. There is also a library exchange for journal articles, with technical libraries in Bratislava, where I can send them lists of journal articles, and they will send it to Germany and if they are published in electronic form I will be given it.'

Orsolya, assistant professor, psychology, Hungary

'I need more of the basic books in my field and that's very hard to get. I just ordered a book from the United States and it's so expensive. When I was a student I was the person who organized the library in the department. And we wrote to some foreign universities to ask them "If you don't need some books, please send them to us", because it's very useful if somebody reads something in the original language.'

Diana, associate professor, education, Portugal

'The last time that I tried to do an interlibrary loan it took me about a month. So I just forgot about it. As a matter of fact I am trying hard to go to Boston to buy books because I need materials and they are not here. I know that they are there, because I go to Amazon on the Internet. Here it is necessary to wait about a month for some and it is not the same as going to the Harvard Bookstore.'

Julie, associate professor, education, Hungary

'Books are a problem, it's very difficult – I buy the books for myself. What I sometimes do is, if it's very expensive, I ask the publisher to send me a copy and I write the review of the book. And now I ask people to send me the manuscript, like chapters if I'm only interested in one chapter, then I ask for it, even before the book has been published if I know that there is work in progress.'

Comment

These comments indicate that in many contexts scholars have difficulties in gaining access to some key resources – notably journal articles, books and book chapters.

Around the world many university libraries have limited budgets or reduced funding, even in well-resourced areas. These scholars indicate that there is a range of alternative ways of accessing necessary resources such as contacting authors directly (usually via email); offering to review books and thus securing a free copy; or travelling to sites where they can collect key materials. Of course the available strategies depend on scholars' economic circumstances: it may be possible for some scholars to travel, for example, to Boston (perhaps by securing a grant), whereas others may rely on colleagues to send them copies of their work – which may depend on being part of academic research networks (see Chapter 12) to know who is doing work on the research they are interested in getting.

10.3 Strategies for funding research writing activities

While obtaining research grants is an issue that scholars across many disciplines face, research funding can make a particular contribution to the academic publishing of multilingual scholars. Read the scholars' comments in Data Example 10.3 and consider these questions: Where have these scholars found sources of grant funding? What resources might these grants provide?

Data Example 10.3: Local and transnational government funding

Joaquim, associate professor, psychology, Portugal

'The last study was funded by the Ministry of Science. Previously I had another grant funded by another agency related to [my research] and now I'm doing another project hoping to be funded by the Ministry of Education, not much money, about five thousand euros. If we have funding, maybe we have someone to work on this project, to collect data, to do everything, money to go abroad then, to do presentations. But if I don't get the funding, I will go on with this project, because I already invested already many hours in this, reading papers and doing meetings. And the motivation is high for everyone so I will not quit if I don't get the grant, but it would be very different, having the grant.'

Fidel, associate professor, education, Spain

Fidel has been involved in several European Union funded research projects with partner institutions from Germany and the Czech Republic. He sees securing such funding as key to building research areas:

'I don't see a *peseta*, penny from the project and I don't need to because I am very well paid as a university lecturer. So I want to work with others because I think we need more people to work on this area, in which more research is needed to improve what is done out there. […] So it's this kind of mediation role in which, on the one side you want to do research to improve the thing; on the other side, part of that research consists of showing others what is being done and how it's working well and all that.'

Such funds not only enable Fidel to employ researchers and to cover costs of attendance at conferences but also to get support with research writing, with monies in some projects dedicated to cover the translation of papers written in Spanish into other languages. Fidel and his team have used such funding in preparing both conference papers and research articles in English.

Comment

As these data extracts show, Joaquim has identified local grant funders who have supported his research, while Fidel has participated in research grants sponsored by the European Union. These grants provide monies for activities supporting scholars' production of texts for publication, as their comments indicate. As Joaquim notes, research grants can include money for hiring staff, traveling to conferences to present research findings and to access other resources discussed in Section 10.2 and on page 99. Fidel's European Union grant likewise provided funds for hiring staff and other material resources related to text production such as the translation of texts into English.

10.4 **Strategies for funding travel**

Traveling to meet and work with colleagues and to attend conferences (Chapter 4) can facilitate scholars' participation in academic research net-

A SCHOLAR'S GUIDE TO GETTING PUBLISHED IN ENGLISH

works (Chapter 12) that can lead to publishing. Read scholars' comments in Data Example 10.4 and consider these questions: How have they managed to get resources for research and travel? What benefits come from gaining access to these resources?

Data Example 10.4: Travel for research and writing activity

Larya, assistant professor, psychology, Slovakia

'The next conference of this association will be held in Glasgow and I've been invited to participate in a symposium there. But I will have to find some money to go to Glasgow. I will have to send the organizers, firstly an abstract and then ask for waiving the conference fee. They did it this way for a conference in the Netherlands – they waived the fee and half the accommodation.'

Martin, associate professor, psychology, Slovakia

'At the end of November we will go to visit [a colleague in the United Kingdom] to speak about our project. We have an Inter-academic Exchange Grant from the British Council. It pays for the accommodation and meals, but not the travel.'

Ornella, assistant professor, psychology, Hungary

'As a post-graduate I went to Spain on a Marie Curie Fellowship for six months. I worked every day in my supervisor's office and he gave me thousands of pages of articles to read. If I had any questions I asked and he answered, and he asked me to read his texts and "please, be critical". I learned a lot from him.'

Diana, associate professor, education, Portugal

'Well the first year that I applied, the dean didn't approve any sabbatical that year. So I applied this year and I got it. Then I applied for a grant at the Science and Technology Foundation and I got it. I proposed a project about [X]. The grant pays for travel expenses, it covers my basic expenses in the United States.'

Ernesto, professor, psychology, Spain

'This month, my student and I will go to [northern Europe] to prepare something together. The university [in northern Europe], they have a project with a general topic of [our research], and they asked us to collaborate. In fact, they have paid for our trip there, because I have no money for that. They have money to pay, in fact, my student will stay there for some months because she will be directly involved in this project. And we will go there again, because they have enough money to do this research.'

Comment

These scholars have found travel funding from a variety of sources. Larya is aware that some conferences (and the associations sponsoring them) recognize the limited financial resources of scholars from certain areas of the world and offer scholarships and waivers or reductions in the cost of the conference and/or housing. Martin, Ornella and Diana have applied for funding available in their local contexts: in Martin's case, a British Council fund for bilateral exchange travel; in Ornella's case, a scholarship for students from European Union member countries; and for Diana, a travel grant from Portugal's Science and Technology Foundation that enabled her to go to the United States for a few months. Ernesto, as an invited partner on a transnational grant, was funded to travel to the northern European country where the lead team works. In most of these cases, while the grants funded only a portion of these scholars' expenses, it was sufficient for them to travel.

10.5 **Thinking about your practice**

1. What books and journals or electronic journal databases are available through your institution? Is the Interlibrary Loan service available – if so, is there a cost? What other ways are there to get bibliographic resources in your context?

2. To what extent do you make work available to others – by sending others copies of your work (or work that you have access to) or by archiving your work in institutional repositories or on open access sites?

3. If you have traveled to conferences in your discipline, whether locally, regionally or transnationally, how have you funded this travel?

4. Have you investigated, applied for, or received fellowships or grants to participate in exchange programs for postgraduates or scholars?

10.6 **Suggestions for future action**

1. Some journals offer reduced rates for subscribers from certain regions of the world. If you review manuscripts for some journals, the publisher may offer you a month's free subscription to their databases. In addition, individual scholars will often send you copies of publications upon request. You can also ask journal book review editors about writing reviews, as the reviewer is allowed to keep the book.

2. Look on conference websites for funding available for scholars from certain regions, students who are willing to help at a conference, and competitive scholarships to attend conferences. Explore whether housing will be offered on university campuses or other institution or if the organizers offer a way for conference attendees to contact each other to share rooms.

3. Websites of institutions, governments or professional associations may announce funding for conference travel, research-related activities, early career scholar fellowships or exchange grants for stays at other institutions.

10.7 **Useful resources**

- Swales, J. and Feak, C. (2011) *Navigating Academia: Writing Supporting Genres.* Ann Arbor: University of Michigan Press. The chapter 'Establishing Yourself in Graduate School' includes sections on writing small grant and fellowship applications.

- Henson, K.T. (2005) *Writing for Publication: Road to Academic Achievement.* Boston, MA: Allyn & Bacon. Chapters 12 to 15 offer detailed advice on finding grants online and writing grant proposals, along with sample proposals.

- Blogs providing country-specific information about sources of funding are increasingly being posted. See, for example, 'The Researchwhisperer', an Australian blog that includes a page on funding research.

10.8 **Related research**

- Mweru, M. (2010) Why Kenyan academics do not publish in international refereed journals. *World Social Science Report: Knowledge Divides* (pp. 110-111). Paris: UNESCO. This chapter reports on the barriers to writing for publication that Kenyan scholars experience, including limited time and material resources.

- Canagarajah, A.S. (1996) Nondiscursive requirements in academic publishing, material resources of periphery scholars, and the politics of knowledge production. *Written Communication* 13 (4), 435-472. This article sketches out the role that limited access to material resources plays in the efforts of scholars in Sri Lanka to publish in centre-based journals.

Information Box 10: Electronic resources

Electronic resources have become increasingly central to academic work and can help scholars in many locations gain access to useful information and opportunities.

List servs are electronic mailing lists focused on particular topics; they may be maintained by formal associations or smaller, informal groups. According to http://www.lsoft.com/catalist.html (where you can search for list servs), there are more than 55,000 publicly available list servs. In some cases, you subscribe to a list serv through a link on an organization's website; some list servs are only for members of an organization, while others are public.

Dissertation/thesis indexes: The Networked Digital Library of Theses and Dissertations is a searchable index of doctoral theses and dissertations, available at http://www.ndltd.org/find.

Blogs (short for 'weblogs') are electronic sites where people or organizations write commentaries on various topics; they may include links to related materials. You can search the Internet for blogs in your discipline or on particular topics. For instance, a list of blogs in the field of social psychology is provided at http://www.socialpsychology.org/blogs.htm.

Bibliographic management programs such as Zotero.com, RefWorks and Endnote can help you keep track of the library resources you use in your research. Some of these are available for free while others charge a fee. Many of these databases allow you to download journal article information, including abstracts, directly from library databases. You can also add notes and comments about texts you have read directly on the database.

Chapter 11

Doing the work of writing in multiple languages

11.1 Chapter focus

When writing texts for publication, scholars adopt a range of approaches to the use of different languages. In this chapter we explore how scholars choose which language to use in writing for different communities and we focus on the approaches and strategies they adopt. Because scholars often conduct research using the local/national language and then write research articles in other languages – often in English – translation may be a key part of text production. Some scholars may use a combination of languages or write in the local/national language. They may then translate their texts themselves or have their texts translated or checked by 'language brokers' (see Chapter 14); other scholars choose to draft texts directly in the language of the target publication, for example, in English for an English-medium journal.

11.2 Tensions in choosing the language of writing

Some multilingual scholars highlight the challenges and tensions between thinking and writing in a local language and writing in another language. Read the views of scholars given in Data Example 11.1 and consider these questions: What do scholars' comments illustrate about the relationship between languages in their writing practices? What issues arise that are important to them?

Data Example 11.1: Writing directly in English

Arturo, assistant professor, psychology, Portugal

'I've been thinking about whether I should write directly in English or write in Portuguese and then translate. Right now I feel that the next article I do, I'll try to write directly in English. It makes more sense to me because I had so many problems with my last article. To translate, to start with, it's a problem. Then the expressions, because even if I try to write in English, I think in Portuguese so the expressions come out in Portuguese and I know some of them. But for some of them I phone my mother [an English teacher] and ask, "How do you say this in English?" And some English grammar is quite different from our grammar.'

Gyorgy, professor, psychology, Hungary

'In the past five or six or maybe ten years it never happened that I wrote a paper in Hungarian and then translated into English, since all of the references, I mean the scientific literature, is in English, so it's much easier to write directly in English. So it takes practice, but you know it involves additional problems because when I finish the first version of the paper in English, I have to restructure the whole piece because in the process that I'm writing the paper in English, I am thinking in Hungarian. Rereading the paper later, I can find a lot of difficulties in the logic of the text, in the structure of the text, and sometimes the paper misses a clear argument.'

Ernesto, professor, psychology, Spain

'The problem, in terms of what do you want to say and how do you want to organize the information and so on, the problem, in my experience, is exactly the same in any language. There I would say that high level processes are exactly the same. Obviously low level processes are different and when I write in English I have an additional problem: how to say this idea? Is it grammatically correct? What I do is to review English papers and learn how people say this or that. I even copy certain expressions that are common in my field, as this is exactly what I want to say.'

Comment

These comments indicate that although, as Ernesto suggests, 'high level' thinking processes may be 'exactly the same', the fact of thinking in one language even while writing in another inevitably complicates the writing process. Indeed, the division between languages in this process is far from straightforward. While some scholars use English as they begin a text, others use both their local language and English at different moments in text production.[1] The comments from these scholars signal the complexity of writing academic texts, as they mention aspects of texts that include argument, structure, logic, particular expressions and different grammars. Scholars' strategies for writing in English include reviewing and revising texts drafted in English, mining English-medium articles for specific phrases to use and asking English-speaking friends (one type of language brokers) for help.

11.3 **The role of translation**

In part because of the complexity of writing academic texts, multilingual scholars vary in how much they use translation as a tool in their writing. They also vary in their perspectives on the usefulness of translation. Read scholars' comments in Data Example 11.2 and consider these questions: How effective do different approaches to translation seem to be for the scholars? What appear to be the advantages and disadvantages of translation?

Data Example 11.2: Approaches to translation

Diana, associate professor, education, Portugal

'I'm a bit tired of this pressure for publishing in English. Now I have just stopped writing directly in English because I realize that it will take much more time and the language was not so good, so now I use Google translator. When I write first in English, because I don't know it well enough, I start to change the language and it turns out to be very basic language and I can't write my ideas in basic language, so with Google's language it's better because the first draft gets done and then I check it. Sometimes it translates word by word and it changes, for instance, the subject, so then I put it in the right way because otherwise it doesn't make sense.'

Larya, assistant professor, psychology, Slovakia

'I had difficulties in my last paper when I had to translate the outcomes of my qualitative research done in Slovak into English and to translate the phrase or certain words that have a certain meaning in Slovak into English and to find the proper phrase for it. […] So I asked my Irish friend to go through it.'

Carla, associate professor, psychology, Spain

'My Spanish co-author and I, we write in English, but we always give the final English manuscript to a private translator, because sometimes there are things that a Spanish native cannot see. She corrects the grammar things which escape me – plurals, or verbs – but she doesn't correct style because she doesn't understand well the context of the work. I always say she has to rely on me for the vocabulary, but the other things besides vocabulary, normally she understands. All the researchers here want to find a native English speaker translator who knows our field, but it's impossible.'

Comment

These scholars all use translation while producing their texts, yet they do so at different points in the text-production process and in different ways: Diana uses machine translation after drafting in Portuguese; after writing an early draft in English, Larya asks an English-speaking friend for help with specific translations; and Carla involves a professional translator toward the end of the writing process. Scholars adopt different strategies for translation, each of which seems to reflect the resources available to them. The question of whether these are effective strategies that lead to successful translations – and publication – is complex. Translation can play a useful role but scholars are keenly aware of its limitations. (In Chapter 14 we explore more fully the work of translators and other 'literacy brokers'.)

11.4 Publishing 'equivalent' texts in different communities

Some scholars aim to publish as much as they can of the texts they write in several languages, for example, publishing in both the local/national language as well as in English to ensure that similar knowledge is made available in both contexts. We call these 'equivalent' versions rather than 'translations', as while there is often considerable overlap in textual versions there are also usually significant differences between them. Figure 11.1 maps the publications by two established scholars, who have worked together for some 40 years, and members of their research team, writing in both Portuguese and English. Look at this figure and consider what it shows about their approach to publishing in Portuguese and English.

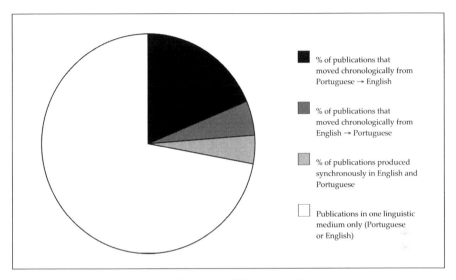

Figure 11.1 Working toward equivalence in publishing in two languages
Adapted from Lillis and Curry (2010), Chapter 5, p. 132.

Comment

*Figure 11.1 indicates that these scholars invest considerable energy in publishing equivalent texts in two languages. Almost one-third of these scholars' publications (of a total of 116) are available in both English **and** Portuguese in different types of publications (journal articles, book chapters and conference proceedings). Of the publications in both languages, 67% were written and published first in Portuguese and then in English; 15% were written first in English and subsequently in Portuguese; and 18% were published in both languages simultaneously, that is, in the same year. The scholars consider that equivalent publishing is crucial if they are to reach the communities to whom they believe research is relevant: they are committed to disseminating their work in Portuguese in the local/national context to contribute to national research and policy; at the same time they are passionate about building their research field transnationally and they consider English to be the linguistic medium which enables them to do this. (See Information Box 11 for concerns and tensions about 'equivalent' publishing.)*

11.5 **Thinking about your practice**

1. Have you had experience using translation for the academic texts you are writing? How did you find the translator and what were the results?

2. What are the costs of translation and other text support services in your context? Are any grants or institutional funds available to pay for translation and other text support services?

3. Have you published 'equivalent' texts for different communities? If so, how did you decide what to include in each text and how to adapt it for different audiences? If not, what are your perspectives on doing so?

11.6 **Suggestions for future action**

1. Compile a list of key phrases and terms from reading published texts to draw on when writing your texts.

2. If you think it would be useful to involve a professional translator or author's editor, ask colleagues for recommendations. It is common before you hire someone to ask to see a work sample and to agree on terms of payment. Translators often charge by the word or page, whereas copyeditors and proofreaders typically charge by the page or the hour, or set a flat rate for a whole project.

3. If you are interested in publishing 'equivalent' texts for different communities (and in different languages), discuss with colleagues their opinions on how this practice is viewed and evaluated in your local context. Also explore the policies on 'first publication' of the journals you are considering submitting to (see Information Box 11).

11.7 **Useful resources**

• The Academic Wordbank at the University of Manchester, UK, provides 'examples of some of the phraseological "nuts and bolts" of writing' used in academic texts: http://www.phrasebank.manchester.ac.uk/index.htm.

- Graff, G. and Birkenstein, C. (2010) *They Say, I Say: The Moves That Matter in Academic Writing* (2nd edn). New York/London: Norton, offers 'templates', or key phrases commonly used in academic texts.

- Swales, J. and Feak, C. (2000) *English in Today's Research World: a writing guide.* Ann Arbor: University of Michigan Press. The first unit, 'The positioning of the research writer', helps readers identify their writing practices, understand 'cross-cultural differences in research languages', and present themselves in biographical statements in publications.

11.8 **Related research**

- Wen, Q. and Gao, Y. (1997) Dual publication and academic inequality. *International Journal of Applied Linguistics* 17 (2), 221-225. The authors explore the situation of Chinese scholars facing the dilemma of which audiences to write for, in which languages, and propose 'dual publication' as a solution.

- *TESOL Quarterly*'s symposium on this topic (2009, 4), including a newer article by Wen and Gao, proposes various solutions including translations, summaries of published research and access to author webpages.

Information Box 11: Policies and tensions in publishing 'equivalent' texts

To reach multiple audiences and broadly disseminate research findings, some scholars publish similar or 'equivalent' texts for different communities. In some contexts there has historically been a strong taboo against publishing the same scholarly work in more than one outlet, often called 'dual publication', particularly if the second publication did not acknowledge the existence of the original publication. This taboo emerged from the view that the main purpose of research is to contribute new knowledge, particularly to the academic community, and therefore a high premium is placed on clearly identifying where something is published for the 'first' time. It is generally much more accepted that research findings may be reformulated or 'translated' into publication of useable suggestions for practice and implications for applied communities, while acknowledging that they originated in research publications, than is publishing for two research audiences. According to the *British Medical Journal*, this type of use is called 'parallel publication' (International Committee of Medical Journal Editors, 1984, 288: 52) and 'occurs when the secondary publication is directed towards a national language group – that is, a target group not (or only to a limited extent) reached by the primary publication. The secondary target group often comprises clinicians who are not likely to use literature retrieval techniques in their professional reading'.

Many journal editors reject the option of equivalent publication because presenting 'new' research findings, often called 'first publication', is seen to increase the status of the journal. In addition, authors typically transfer copyright to the journal when an article is published, so they technically don't 'own' the text from that point and must seek permission to reuse it in subsequent publications. A more generally accepted use of dual publication includes reprinting previously published texts with full acknowledgement and permission of the original source; for example, journal articles may be reprinted in edited books.

In addition to the valuing of 'first publication' by journal editors, institutional evaluation systems in many contexts also discourage dual/equivalent publishing, with some viewing the practice as 'self-plagiarising' or unethically copying one's own work. However, the taboo against dual publication has typically functioned in contexts where both publications appear in the same language. As the strong taboo position does not take into account the many potential communities that multilingual scholars may want and need to address, or the fact that many 'equivalent' texts do not cover exactly the same content, some scholars have proposed a reconsideration of the taboo. Indeed, Chinese scholars Wen and Gao (2007) argue for the acceptance of 'dual publication' as a means to redress the inequality perpetuated by strict interpretations of the notion of 'first' or 'prior' publication for multilingual scholars with restricted access to the global academic marketplace. Whether scholars can disseminate 'equivalent' publications appears to depend on how flexible and open might be the editors of journals and other publications. Scholars who achieve dual publication usually seek permission from journals when they wish to publish a version of an existing paper in another language, whether in a journal or an edited book.

Note

1   Of course the processes are actually more complex than this, given that any 'language' is actually a cluster of varieties and features.

Chapter 12

Participating in academic research networks

12.1 Chapter focus

One way to gain access to the social and material resources (see Chapter 9) needed to support text production, and to identify opportunities for publishing, is by participating in local and transnational networks. Scholars enter or create networks in a variety of ways, including collaborating with local colleagues as well as colleagues from a range of contexts, attending conferences and making connections through virtual means (e.g. social media, email). Through network participation scholars can gain access to various resources and make contributions to networks, depending on what they can offer. As this chapter explores, scholars also play a range of roles in networks, including that of 'network broker' – people who play a central role and can help others gain access to networks.[1]

12.2 Understanding what networks can offer

Data Example 12.1 specifies some of the resources that can be accessible to scholars through participation in networks. Look at this list and consider these questions: What kinds of resources can be available through networks and how do these interrelate?

Data Example 12.1: Resources available through networks

Contacts (connections to other scholars, both local and distant)
Information (about local and transnational conferences, grants, publishing opportunities)
Academic materials, such as journal articles
Rhetorical resources (e.g. English-language writing expertise and assistance)
Collaboration on writing (including in English)
Collaboration on research (including the full spectrum of research and writing activities)
Brokering (e.g. connections to publishing opportunities, support with writing and publishing, help in interpreting reviewers' comments, etc.)

(From Lillis & Curry, 2010, Figure 3.2)

Comment

The social nature of networks is valuable in itself: being in contact with other scholars linked to your field, both locally and transnationally, provides opportunities for intellectual exchange that can be academically exciting and personally satisfying. Getting access to, and building relationships with, other scholars can help you secure access to important material resources such as articles and books, as well as less tangible resources such as information about opportunities for funding, conferences and publishing; connections to other academics; and the potential for collaboration on research, writing and editing.

12.3 Developing a transnational network

A key way to understand networks is from the perspective of scholars who participate in them. Data Example 12.2 provides information on how one scholar forged such a network. Read the case study and consider these questions: How did Larya develop access to and participate in networks? What benefits has she received from participating in these networks?

Data Example 12.2: Slovak psychology scholar Larya's transnational network

While she was a student, Larya's PhD supervisor suggested that she contact an Austrian professor in her discipline located relatively close by. She visited the professor three times in Austria then kept in touch with her:

'[The Austrian professor] is in contact with other people working in the psychology of [X] abroad and she gave me some guidelines on, or advice about, who to contact if I have a certain problem.'

From the Austrian professor Larya learned about a conference in the Netherlands. She attended the conference, where 'I found more contacts and I'm not some "big foreigner", but now in a community.' At the conference she learned about a scholar who works in Belgium, whom she later met at another conference in Germany. They discussed the possibility of her doing a research stay at his university if she could get a grant from a Slovak organization. Larya applied for and received the grant and spent four months at the scholar's university in Belgium working with him and others. Supported by discussions with this scholar, Larya drafted an article which was published in an English-medium Slovak journal. After Larya returned to Slovakia she stayed in contact with her colleagues in Belgium.

Comment

Larya developed this network by following her supervisor's suggestion to make contact with the Austrian scholar, who then gave her information about the conference in the Netherlands. There she heard about a scholar from Belgium and met him later in Germany, where they discussed her coming to his university. By developing these transnational ties, Larya learned about scholars in her sub-discipline, relevant conferences and financial resources to support an extended stay in another country, all of which led to her getting published. As noted in Chapter 4, Larya also gained intellectually from presenting at these conferences and learned about possible target journals.

12.4 **Network development over time**

Academic research networks change and develop (or decay) over time as scholars' interests, experiences and connections change. Look at the two network diagrams presented in Data Example 12.3 and consider these questions: Which parts of Larya's networks have been maintained over time? Which parts are new? What conclusions can you draw from seeing her networks at two different moments?

Data Example 12.3: Larya's networks in 2002 and 2007

In 2002, while working on her PhD, Larya began to develop her network, as indicated in Figure 12.1. Figure 12.2 shows her network some years later. In the two network diagrams provided here Larya is situated at the center, with her strong ties to others indicated by solid lines and weak ties indicated by dotted lines.

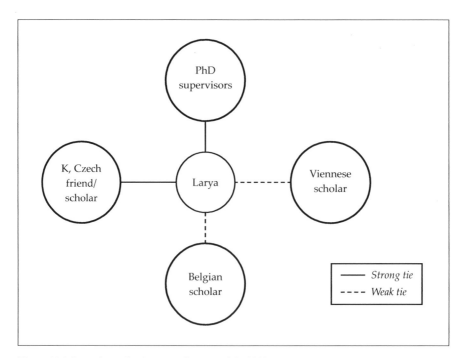

Figure 12.1 Larya's academic research network in 2002

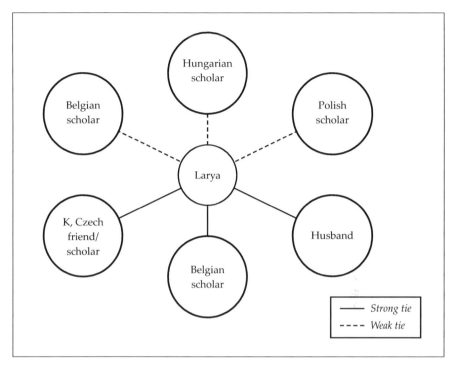

Figure 12.2 Larya's academic research network in 2007, three years post-PhD

Comment

In the later (2007) network diagram (Figure 12.2) Larya's network is larger than her earlier network; it shows strong ties to the Belgian scholars with whom Larya worked for four months and to K, her colleague in the Czech Republic. It also shows newer (weak) ties to a scholar she met during an inter-university exchange in Poland (which resulted in publishing a book chapter); ties to other scholars in the Czech Republic and a scholar in Hungary (all of whom she collaborated with on a grant application to a regional foundation); and strong ties to a local scholar (who is also her husband). Absent from Larya's 2007 network diagram are her PhD supervisors, partly because her research focus had shifted, and the Viennese professor. In addition, Larya expanded her network by traveling to various conferences and pursuing opportunities to collaborate with others. Mapping out Larya's network at two moments in times helps us understand how her network grew and changed and supported her publishing activity.

12.5 **Roles and contributions to academic networks**

In the network history in Data Example 12.4 we explore the contributions made by members of local and transnational networks to an article co-published by Istvan, a Hungarian professor who works in both psychology and medicine departments, and his students and colleagues. Read the network history and look at the diagram in Figure 12.3. Consider these questions: What is Istvan's position in this network? What do his actions in the production of the text tell you about his role? What position in the network does Istvan occupy? How does this position enable him to mobilize the resources that members of his network can offer in doing research, drafting text and preparing a manuscript for submission to a journal?

Data Example 12.4: Text production in/as networked activity

Istvan's chief and longest-lasting research network began in 1997 when two U.S. researchers read an article he had published and invited him to visit them. Istvan has since co-authored seven articles with these colleagues. The activity in this text history took place over three years and resulted in the publication of an article in a British journal with his local students and colleagues as co-authors.

Stage 1: Istvan, with one of his psychology undergraduate students (Tibor in Figure 12.3), and two post-doctoral researchers in his laboratory (KL and BK in Figure 12.3), conducted experiments with female students as research subjects, using the Hungarian language. Istvan had previously developed these experimental methods with the U.S. colleagues (WK and LM in Figure 12.3). To report the results of these collaborative experiments, Istvan drafted an article in English with Tibor's help, as Tibor's control of English was better than Istvan's. After feedback from his colleague WK, Istvan submitted the manuscript to an 'international' English-medium journal. The article was rejected at that point, primarily because only female subjects were included in the experiments.

Stage 2: In response, Istvan secured funding for Tibor to conduct the experiments, this time using male subjects. Istvan drew on the new findings to rewrite the article and sent this version to WK, who suggested detailed changes to the text. Istvan submitted the revision to another English-medium 'international' journal, which accepted the article pending changes. After Istvan enlisted Tibor's help in making these revisions, the article was published. All of the contributors – Istvan, Tibor, the two post-doctoral researchers and two U.S. colleagues – were named authors.

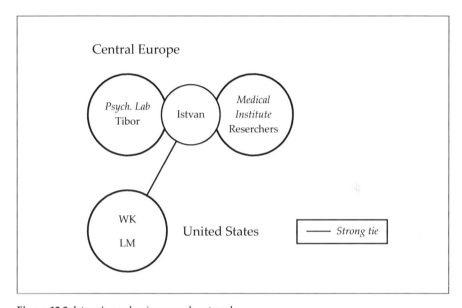

Figure 12.3 Istvan's academic research network

Text history and network diagram adapted from Lillis and Curry (2006b).

Comment

It is clear from the diagram and the text history that Istvan plays a pivotal role in this network, a role we describe as 'network broker' in that he brokers the involvement of his student and post-doctoral fellows into his transnational network, thereby providing publishing opportunities for local network members. Members of this transnational network made different contributions to the research and the article. Locally, Tibor played a major role in conducting experiments, analyzing results and supporting English-medium writing. Post-doctoral fellows KL and BK also contributed to conducting the research. WK, a US colleague, added scientific, linguistic and rhetorical knowledge that helped Istvan shape the article for eventual publication.

12.6 **Thinking about your practice**

1. Do you participate in research groups, seminar series or other meetings of colleagues in your local context or beyond? If so, what do you contribute to them? What do you take away?

2. Who plays a pivotal role in the transnational networks that you are aware of? Do you have a connection to these 'network brokers'?

3. Do you act as a network broker for others, whether in your local or transnational networks?

12.7 **Suggestions for future action**

1. Make contact with other researchers, local or transnational, who are doing work related to yours so you can exchange ideas and perhaps develop collaborations. You can do this by speaking with conference presenters about their work or making connections electronically (email addresses may be available in scholars' publications, personal or institutional websites or on the Internet).

2. As you begin to work together discuss your various contributions. Participants in networks may have different ideas about the purposes of collaborating, and the roles, tasks and responsibilities of networks members. Identify what you hope to contribute and gain from participating in a network in order to foster successful collaboration.

3. If you are a student, consider participating in formal student networks sponsored by local universities, government or regional agencies or scholarly associations. Attending e-fora (electronic forums), summer schools and doctoral seminars is another way to meet people. At conferences, take advantage of events and sessions aimed specifically at postgraduates or early career scholars.

12.8 **Useful resources**

- Boden, R., Kenway, J. and Epstein, D. (2007) *Building Networks*. London: Sage. Part of the Academic's Support Kit, this book offers suggestions on how to build and sustain academic networks.

- Agre, P. (2002) *Networking on the Network: A Guide to Professional Skills for PhD Students* provides advice on using electronic media to engage in academic networks and includes an extensive bibliography: http://vlsicad. ucsd.edu/Research/Advice/network.html (accessed 15 February 2013).

- **Vitae.ac.uk** is an 'organisation championing the personal, professional and career development of doctoral researchers and research staff in higher education institutions and research institutes' based in the United Kingdom. Its Postgraduate Research page has a posting, 'Networking at Conferences', that offers tips on making connections.

12.9 **Related research**

- Ferenz, O. (2005) EFL writers' social networks: impact on advanced academic literacy development. *Journal of English for Academic Purposes* 4 (4), 339-351. This article traces the influence of social networks on the language choice of Israeli postgraduates as they write in different genres.

- Ordóñez-Matamoros, H.G., Cozzens, S.E., and García, M. (2010) International co-authorship and research team performance in Colombia. *Review of Policy Research* 27 (4), 415-431. This bibliometric and interview study demonstrates that scientists in Colombia who co-authored with partners located in other countries increased their output by 40% and were more likely to involve their local research teams in the collaboration than those who did not collaborate transnationally.

Information Box 12: Academic research networks

Within the competitive economy of knowledge production, scholars' participation in academic research networks can enable them to mobilize resources
essential for publishing. Networks can be characterized as formal or informal,
with formal networks often resulting from top-down initiatives from, for example, geopolitical regions such as the European Union and the Association
of South-East Asian Nations or global institutions such as the World Bank.
These initiatives may include incentives or funding aimed at increasing research output through collaboration. However, research suggests that formal
networks created in this way seem to be less powerful than personally created
or informally generated local networks (also see Defazio, Lockett & Wright,
2009; Melin, 2000). Less formal but still organized networks may be connected
with academic associations, such as Special Interest Groups (SIGS). Within
these loosely organized networks individual members may meet and connect
through activities of a SIG; however, such groups are not likely to offer funding or other material support (though they may have places reserved for them
on conference programs).

Networks can also be considered local or transnational. In contrast to the
externally established networks created by supranational organizations or academic associations' SIGS, which may be transnational, local networks have
an important role in supporting access to the resources needed for scholarly
publishing, including brokering links to transnational networks. In addition,
local networks are often stronger and more durable than transnational networks and participation in them appears to benefit scholars in terms of conducting and disseminating research and building local research structures.

At the same time, scholars can face difficulties in participating in and sus-
taining networks, which depend on, but go beyond, material resources. For
example, scholars who attend conferences or SIG meetings may still have uneven access to making connections with key network brokers. If, as Katz and
Martin claim, 'most collaborations begin informally and are often the result
of informal conversation' (1997: 4), it is important for scholars to feel comfortable with making personal connections. Ideally, those who are already established within networks would act as brokers facilitating such connections.
Thus some of the burden of making network connections falls on scholars'
shoulders, but not everyone has access to network brokers or members, or
feels comfortable interacting with them. Some scholars develop their contributions to networks by helping to organize local, regional and transnational
conferences or by communicating with others through electronic communications. (Adapted from Curry & Lillis, 2010.)

Note

1   For more on network brokers, see Curry and Lillis (2010a).

Chapter 13

Collaborating on texts for publication

13.1 **Chapter focus**

In recent years, both collaboration on research activities and the co-authorship of academic publications have increased globally, perhaps because of growing pressure to publish and greater opportunities for virtual communication. Co-authoring, however, may be more or less common depending on scholars' disciplines, institutional reward systems and personal preferences. Co-authoring practices include researchers working together, supervisors writing with postgraduate students, students collaborating with each other, and researchers from local and transnational teams collaborating on specific tasks. There are often both benefits and drawbacks to co-authoring, so it can be useful to consider various aspects before embarking on a specific project. It's also important to bear in mind that in many contexts scholars may be under pressure to publish single-authored articles, thereby meeting evaluation criteria that measure academic achievement in terms of individual research and writing activity, or to be first author (or in some disciplines, the last) on collaborative publications. In this chapter we explore the practices of co-authoring texts for publication and the issues that can arise.

13.2 **Collaboration with colleagues**

Worldwide, collaboration and co-authoring are increasingly common practices between colleagues in local, regional and transnational networks. After reading the accounts in Data Example 13.1 consider this question: In what ways do scholars support each other in writing and revising texts for publication?

Data Example 13.1: Enlisting a colleague's critical eye

Julie, associate professor, education, Hungary

'I have a colleague here, I learned a lot from her and she's a very critical person [...] even if she doesn't understand the topic I show my writing to her and she has very good comments. Like with my book, I asked her specifically please underline every sentence you have to read twice and she did that for me. And now we work together on some things.'

Ernesto, professor, psychology, Spain

'Pierre [a long-time collaborator in France] and I have published a number of papers and in all the cases the procedure is the same. In some of the papers Pierre was the main author and in the other cases I wrote the paper. In some cases we have done a lot of revision. I remember especially one of the papers, I sent my comments to Pierre after receiving his comments. Then he sent everything back to me and I wrote quite a lot, two pages of comments and so on. We are very fluent in communicating if you say, well, I think maybe you should change this, or you should be more specific in this or that.'

Comment

In these accounts Julie emphasizes the value of gaining another scholar's critical perspective on her writing. She illustrates how, in this case, an ongoing working relationship evolved from one of support (or literacy brokering – see Chapter 14) to one of co-authoring. Ernesto's comments pinpoint the different responsibilities that he and his long-term collaborator tend to take – each one sometimes taking a leading or a secondary role in co-authoring particular texts. These extracts demonstrate the range of roles that can be played by colleagues who are co-authors in a long-term collaboration as well as those who are not co-authors but provide critical feedback on a manuscript. These comments also illustrate the interpersonal nature of communicating about the work. The scholars' comments suggest the need for honesty and trust in communicating with colleagues about possible revisions to texts – and how collaborations may change at different moments in time.

13.3 Collaboration between supervisors and students

Some scholars supervising master's and doctoral students engage in different ways of writing for publication with their students. Read the range of comments in Data Example 13.2 and consider this question: What might be the benefits and drawbacks of supervisors and students writing together for publication – from the perspectives of both supervisor and student?

Data Example 13.2: Writing with students

Diana, associate professor, education, Portugal

'In this project, I have a master's thesis student. She finished her thesis already and it is very good and we produced together, two papers. Then last summer, there was an international meeting in Porto and I was invited to coordinate a working group on [X] and so we presented a paper about that research. And then there was a national seminar and we presented the material. And there will be an edited book, it's not a proceedings, and so we are doing a chapter for that text.'

Inês, associate professor, education, Portugal

'When [my colleague and I] supervise a thesis we are recognised as being very strict, but in fact when students finish their doctoral thesis we feel comfortable because we could get good work and could publish several papers from the thesis with the student, because our supervising is very close to the students and they help show to us what has happened in the data. We construct the instruments with them, we do research with them.'

Julie, associate professor, education, Hungary

'I actually learned how to publish from my PhD supervisor and it was he who pushed me to publish, so without him I wouldn't have, because of low self-confidence. . . . if it wasn't for [him], I wouldn't have ever started publishing because I thought I'm not clever enough for that kind of thing. And then when he left [the country], for a long time he still read some of my papers and we wrote things together.'

Rebeca, assistant professor, psychology, Spain

'[My former supervisor] is always telling me that I tend to write one argument and then another argument. So I have to write with more clarity and
shorter sentences, trying to find better-cohering arguments so everything
is clear from the beginning, so results and methods come as a consequence
of the theoretical introduction. I have learned from writing this paper and
after doing the PhD and there has been an advance with the help from [my
supervisor].'

Arturo, assistant professor, psychology, Portugal

'[My supervisor] used us [postgraduate students] to make the posters for presentations. He likes to think and to talk and to write about conversations and
about science, about psychology, about education, but he does not like com-
puters. He's an experienced communicator, but I can't remember having those
kinds of tutorials about papers, making posters, or communications. He wrote
in Portuguese and asked me to translate or made someone else translate.'

Jirina, assistant professor, psychology, Slovakia

'I was a little angry when I wrote with Dana [my supervisor] because I was
used to writing something, and it's finished or it's complete, when I write the
last sentence it's okay. And then I worked with Dana and there was again and
again having to write in a different way and again different and again and I
wrote it with her about four months, […] very long, very long, and I was really tired. But for this I am more sure that it is better than previous papers.
They were just like a first draft and this case was really where it changed.'

Comment

*These comments show the range of experiences scholars have had in collaborating
on textual production as both supervisors and students. Supervisors may benefit
from increasing their publications output, and, as in the case of Diana, in building
network connections leading to publishing opportunities. Supervisors who collaborate with the students whose research and writing abilities they have fostered, as
with Inês and her colleague, can also benefit from co-authoring papers for publication. As students themselves, scholars recall receiving help that bolstered their confi-
dence and material support through having supervisors read and comment on their
manuscripts – but they also have had experiences like the scholar who supported his*

supervisor's professional activities without feeling he learned very much. Scholars working with students tend to introduce students to some of the key aspects of the hard work of writing for publication: the investment of considerable time and effort and the patience to return to a text to make multiple revisions over time. As with any human enterprise, collaboration can sometimes be frustrating for those involved, but it also offers the potential for learning and increased publishing production.

13.4 **Thinking about your practice**

1. Are most publications in your (sub)discipline single authored, co-authored or some of each? If co-authored, how many authors typically collaborate on a published text?

2. How do your institutional evaluation criteria reward co-authored publications as compared with other publications?

3. Have you had experience collaborating on a text in your local language or in English? If so, what were your contributions and the contributions of other people? Who initiated the collaboration? What did each collaborator contribute?

4. If you have not had this experience, what knowledge and abilities could you offer to a potential collaboration? Where could you use help? Who could you approach to discuss the possibility of collaborating? Where could you get advice on how to establish a productive collaboration?

13.5 **Suggestions for future action**

1. Consider who might be potential collaborators in your institution, as well as in any of your local, regional and transnational networks. Who do you know who shares your interests? Who could contribute what to a joint project?

2. Try to identify the aspects of academic writing in which you feel more or less confident or experienced. Think about possible collaborators who could complement your strengths and weaknesses.

3. Discuss with colleagues and supervisors how single versus co-authored publications are viewed and rewarded in your context. How do these scholars balance writing alone with collaborating on texts, if they do?

13.6 **Useful resources**

* Lunsford, A. and Ede, L. (2012) *Writing Together: Collaboration in Theory and Practice*. New York: Bedford/St. Martin's. This retrospective book includes a section, 'Why write together?'

* Thomson, P. and Kamler, B. (2012) *Writing for Peer Reviewed Journals: Strategies for Getting Published*. London: Routledge, also discuss collaboration in Chapter 8, 'Writing Together'.

* The Researchwhisperer blog includes posts on co-authoring: http://theresearchwhisperer.wordpress.com/tag/co-writing/. (Accessed 10 August 2013).

* For tips on collaboration, see 'Author, author, author: Effective collaborative writing' at http://allcollaboration.squarespace.com/home/2010/2/15/author-author-author-effective-collaborative-writing.html.

13.7 **Related research**

* Braine, G. (2005) The challenge of academic publishing: a Hong Kong perspective. *TESOL Quarterly* 39 (4), 707-716. This study explores English-medium publishing by applied linguistics scholars in Hong Kong, considering co-authoring and gatekeeping practices.

* Akkerman, S., Admiraal, W., Simons, R.J. and Niessen, T. (2006) Considering diversity: multivoicedness in international academic collaboration. *Culture and Psychology* 12, 461-485. This study of a collaboration by scholars from Scotland, Italy, Denmark, the Netherlands and Spain shows that while diversity should be seen as a resource for international collaboration, it also needs to be actively addressed in interactions.

Information Box 13: Collaborating and co-authoring

Collaboration can be a result of participating in academic research networks. However collaboration develops, it can be useful to consider various aspects of co-authoring and discuss these with potential collaborators before you begin to work together in the hopes of forestalling problems or delays. If you are working on a project directed by someone else, you may have already discussed the ethical and practical issues related to publishing, such as:

- the order of authors named on the paper (see below);
- who will make which specific contributions to the project/text;
- how much time each collaborator has to devote to the joint project;
- what schedules and deadlines are mutually agreeable – and feasible;
- which journal the paper will be submitted to first and which other journals might be suitable targets if necessary.

If you are instigating a writing collaboration you may wish to bring up these issues as well as considering which collaborators might bring complementary strengths to the project and what might hinder the successful completion of a collaboration.

Order of authorship: In most academic disciplines the first author is the person who contributes the most to a text, but in some cases the first author might be a project director, with the rest of the authors listed in an order that indicates their relative contributions – in addition to writing, these contributions may include conceptualizing the project, reviewing literature and doing methodological work. In some disciplines the project or laboratory director is listed last, signalling a position as the leader. In other cases authors may list their names in alphabetical order; in still other cases authors may alternate order of names on multiple co-authored publications (in these last two cases a footnote may explain these choices). It is important to note that because evaluation systems usually measure success in terms of *individual* outputs, scholars sometimes make strategic agreements about claiming first or leading authorship of a paper.

Seemingly mundane decisions about collaboration can be important to successful co-authoring, including reaching agreement about the following questions:

- Who will draft which parts of a text? Who will create figures, tables, or other graphics?
- How and when will co-authors make comments or edits on each other's texts?
- What are each co-author's preferences/habits for writing versus editing at different stages of the text-production process?
- How will communication take place about the text as it develops, particularly if co-authors are in different locations?

- How and where will drafts of texts be stored and how will changes made to the most recent version be noted (for example, systems for dating drafts, using electronic editing features such as Track Changes in Microsoft Word™, using internet programs such as Google Docs and Dropbox that give multiple authors access to documents).
- Who will check that all references are included, accurate and corresponding to citations in the text?
- Who will check that the article is formatted according to the journal's guidelines or other formats, such as APA or Harvard?
- Who will get copyright permissions for any material to be reprinted in the publication?
- Who will be the 'corresponding author', the person who submits the final text to a journal, receives correspondence from gatekeepers, is responsible for sending changes to a journal and collating corrections on proof copies of the typeset article (see Information Box 9)?

Chapter 14

Getting help from literacy brokers

14.1 Chapter focus

Whilst it is often assumed that academic texts are produced by individual scholars or – in some disciplines – by groups of scholars, in fact many other people are often also involved. In preparing texts for publication – particularly when writing in several languages – scholars call on people for different kinds of help and support. We refer to such people as 'literacy brokers' and have identified two key types: *academic brokers,* such as colleagues in a scholar's discipline who tend to orient their feedback to research content, methodology and the conversations of the discipline; and *language brokers*, such as translators, authors' editors or – in the context of writing English-medium texts – other people with knowledge of English (teachers, friends and relatives) who tend to orient their feedback to the structure, format and language of texts. Such brokering is an important, if often invisible, aspect to successful academic text production: identifying which kinds of support or brokering might be useful at different stages of writing can help you produce a successful text.[1]

14.2 Scholars' perspectives on what brokers can offer

In this section we present the views of multilingual scholars that illustrate how academic and language brokers can help in text production – and some limitations to the support they can give. Read their comments and consider these questions: What kinds of support do you see as being offered from different types of brokers? Where might the support provided by academic and language brokers overlap?

Data Example 14.1: Benefits and drawbacks of involving brokers

Gyorgy, professor, psychology, Hungary

'It's not easy to find out which kind of style or logic is necessary for writing a paper properly. For example, I submitted a paper to a journal, they rejected it, and then I requested one of my colleagues who lives in [the United Kingdom where] I spent one year. [...] I asked him to contribute to this paper, he corrected it, not too deeply, and we sent it to another journal. It was accepted right away, which means that that he was aware of the necessary cultural knowledge, necessary scientific techniques and the necessary styles, including grammar.'

Martin, associate professor, psychology, Slovakia

'Now when we did a common project with our UK partner, probably he knew before the process that there may be five journals which are good or to which we can realistically send our product.'

Ornella, assistant professor, psychology, Hungary

'Because my aunt is an English teacher and not an expert in psychology, sometimes she didn't understand the scientific meaning of the sentence. She found mistakes that I made in agreement of plural and singular forms. But even though she speaks very good English and spent some years in England, she's not familiar with the academic terms and she uses words in a different way.'

Comment

Both Gyorgy and Martin demonstrate a keen awareness of what their UK colleagues have contributed to their collaborations – Gyorgy notes his colleague's 'cultural knowledge, necessary scientific techniques and the necessary styles' of academic writing, while Martin points to his collaborator's deep familiarity with potential target journals. In contrast, Ornella notes the limitations of her aunt's knowledge of the types of academic language that Ornella needs to use in journal articles. While both academic and language brokers in these examples provide some assistance with language, it is the academic brokers who also provide broader knowledge of the discipline, such as target journals and their preferences. However, the distinction between 'language' and 'content' is not straightforward and, as mentioned above, brokers often comment on both aspects but tend to emphasize one or the other, as is illustrated in the text examples in the next section.

14.3 Textual interventions by academic literacy brokers before and after submission

The data discussed in Section 14.2 focused on scholars' texts before submitting them to journals for review. However, literacy brokering takes place both before and after submission for publication. Consider Data Example 14.2, which involves changes made to a draft of an article. What kind of changes did the broker make [as indicated by the tracked changes]?

Data Example 14.2: Working with brokers before submission

When looking at [?] the highest educational qualification obtained by the participants,

in the Prague random sample there are more people with general high school qualifica-

tion (31,8%) than in the Bratislava random sample (22,7%). [...] We could say that the

target group participants are more middle-class than the random sample participants

[isn't this a bit problematic What do you mean by middle class?].

Comment

In this example the broker inserted comments and changes that signal his orientation to both language and content. The two insertions of 'the' may be seen as straightforward additions of the definite article (a language change); his question mark after the insertion of 'at' shows that even seemingly small grammatical changes (the insertion of a preposition) can raise meaningful choices for writers and brokers; the longer comment about the characterization of participants as 'middle-class' points to the broker's understanding of disciplinary conversations about terminology ('Isn't this a bit problematic. What do you mean by middle class?').

Data Example 14.3 presents some of the post-submission feedback that Portuguese education scholar Diana received on her book chapter manuscript (discussed in Chapter 8) from the Portuguese book co-editor. Read the reviews and consider this question: How did the co-editor of the book evaluate Diana's manuscript?

Data Example 14.3: Extracts from the co-editor's review

1. Focus and rationale of the paper: The focus on [X] is clear in the abstract and in the Introduction. The rationale is also clear. But chapters in [the publisher's books] have no abstract. Thus, the information you need must all be in the text.

2. Theoretical framework: The section [providing background] is very useful for international readers. Information is needed about the Portuguese context. The theoretical frame is clear but I missed a clear definition of [key terms] – does this mean the same in all cultures? – and other key constructs used in the frame. Several corrections according to APA norms must be done.

3. Method: There is some information about the research but it is not explicit (1) that this is an interpretative and ethnographic approach – as far as I understood; 2) that this is a case study – also as far as I understood. The paradigm and type of research should be clearly stated. There is some information about the participants but it is not enough. Namely it is not clear why this community was chosen as object of this study–why this particular one and not another one also with [similar demographic characteristics].

   The data collecting instruments reported are only participant observation. How was it registered? By photos? Videos? In a researcher's diary? If the observation lasted two years there should be some kind of registration tool. And was it just the observation? No informal conversations? No interviews? No document analysis? It is not clear for the reader how the research was really conducted. There is also no information about data treatment and analysis. This should also be provided.

4. Results: Are the most interesting section of the chapter. They are rich and well supported in evidence. If some more examples were given they would even become more appealing – I mean, before the cases. The 4 cases are very illuminating. They provide adequate evidence.

5. Final/Concluding remarks: They are adequate to the research and results.

6. Clarity: The English language needs some improvements. Please consider the suggestions of the native English speaker reviewers. They did a very careful job (see the text and suggestions enclosed).

7. Relevance to this BOOK: Very relevant. This chapter focuses on an important topic for this book – [X]. But I would say that as the book title is [X], part of [X] is very well addressed in the chapter, but the role of [Y] should be made more clear (e.g. what characterizes [X] in this kind of [participant]? And of [other contexts]?)

Final remarks – References – for a chapter published in 2008 having just two or three references from 2002 and the others much older than that does not seem adequate. Suggestion: add some more updated references. The references should follow the APA norms. This correction must be done very carefully.

Please – Read and use the [publisher's] norms before sending the final version of the chapter. Chapters can have a maximum of 28 pages.

Comment

The numbered sections in the review suggest how the editor is evaluating the chapter (1. focus and rationale of the paper; 2. theoretical framework; 3. methods; 4. results; 5. conclusions; 6. clarity of writing; 7. relevance to the overall book project; 8. additional comments). The book co-editor recommended that Diana integrate the abstract into the chapter; provide definitions in the theoretical framework; explain her research methods; and clarify the writing and update references. Thus as an academic literacy broker, the book co-editor mainly emphasized content but also mentioned language and writing concerns; here again, brokering is a complex activity involving responding to text production – and publishing practices – in multiple ways at the same time.

Data Examples 14.4a and 14.4b display two parts of the feedback from a peer reviewer of Diana's chapter (see Information Box 14) – the covering letter and an extract of the reviewer's editing of her manuscript. Consider this feedback and these questions: What main overall changes were suggested by the peer reviewer in Data Example 14.4a for Diana to revise her chapter? What do you notice about the textual changes proposed in Data Example 14.4b?

Data Example 14.4a: Report on Diana's chapter by a peer reviewer

'This is an excellent chapter in my view – interesting case studies that reveal the place of schooling in [X]. I worked hard on the editing. The figures need to be structured better (I didn't try to do that). The text is written clearly and in fact in a quite complex way (the meaning is always clear) but the English needed a lot of small editing. I hope it helps.'

Data Example 14.4b: Reviewer's comments on an extract from the manuscript [using the track changes feature]

Extract of original text, with reviewer's proposed changes	Extract of revised text with changes accepted by the author
This study suggests that the State must stimulate civic participation, and help to create a strong sense and practice of citizenship if schooling and other educational processes are to transform students' lives. In addition, schools should systematically promote discussions with the community and participation in community activities. Schools ought to comprehend the multiplicity of reasons for failure, as well as to facilitate the dialogue between school and families to provide families with real possibilities of participation in their children's success.	This study suggests that the State must stimulate civic participation, and help to create a strong sense and practice of citizenship if schooling and other educational processes are to transform students' lives. In addition, schools should systematically promote discussions with the community and participation in community activities. Schools ought to comprehend the multiplicity of reasons for failure, as well as to facilitate the dialogue between school and families to provide families with real possibilities of participation in their children's success.

Comment

While this brief, positive review in Data Example 14.4a did not offer substantive comments on Diana's chapter, it was accompanied by a copy of the manuscript which the reviewer had closely edited (and characterised as 'a lot of small editing'), as shown in Data Example 14.4b. The revised text after the reviewer's changes is considerably shorter than the original, omitting the repetition of background information at the beginning of the text and some of the more theoretical language in the original version (e.g. 'Therefore, in a context where the historical memory of schooling …'). Thus language brokering can take place on multiple levels, from removing theoretical language to making mechanical changes, for example, from the plural 'communities' to the singular 'community' in the last sentence.

14.4 Thinking about your practice

1. What kinds of support would help you in writing texts for publication?

2. Who do you, or could you, ask to read your manuscripts in progress and give you feedback on them? Who do you help with their manuscripts?

3. Have you worked with academic and/or language brokers? If so, what were your experiences with receiving and responding to feedback?

4. Where might you find different types of brokers to work with on your texts? How could you approach them and specify the kinds of support you would find useful?

14.5 Suggestions for future action

1. Consider how to engage with academic literacy brokers in ways that recognize the shortage of time in scholars' work lives. Could brokers provide helpful feedback that might not involve reading an entire manuscript?

2. Ask colleagues if your institution has funds for language support or, if your research is funded, whether the grant provides funds to hire language brokers. However, because language brokers often may lack

knowledge of your discipline, it is important to evaluate their suggestions carefully.

3. Think about ways that you can collaborate with others (peers, colleagues, supervisors) to provide brokering support.

14.6 **Useful resources**

- Nygaard, L. (2008) *Writing for Scholars: A Practical Guide to Making Sense and Being Heard.* Oslo: Universitetsforlaget/Copenhagen Business School Press/Liber, Chapter 8, 'Holding up the mirror: Giving and receiving feedback,' prepares writers to respond to interventions from literacy brokers.

- The document, *Peer review: The nuts and bolts,* is available from the Sense about Science website (http://www.senseaboutscience.org/resources.php/ 99/peer-review-the-nuts-and-bolts; accessed 08 November, 2012).

- Materese, V. (ed.) (2013) *Supporting Research Writing: Roles and Challenges in Multilingual Settings.* Cambridge, UK: Chandos Publishing includes chapters exploring the practices of those who support academic writers (such as translators and editors), including multilingual scholars.

14.7 **Related research**

- Englander, K. (2008) Revision of scientific manuscripts by nonnative-English-speaking scientists in response to journal editors' criticism of the language. *Journal of Applied Linguistics* 3 (2), 129-161. This article demonstrates how Mexican scholars' revisions to texts in response to literacy brokers' feedback changed not only the language but also the positioning of the scientists in relation to the journal's audience.

- Gosden, H. (1995) Success in research article writing and revision: A social-constructionist perspective. *English for Specific Purposes* 14 (1), 37-57. Gosden examines the revisions made to articles published by multilingual scholars as a result of interactions with colleagues and literacy broker gatekeepers.

Information Box 14: Peer review

Peer review is one of the main ways that manuscripts are evaluated, in principle by knowledgeable scholars in the discipline (considered 'peers' of the author). Journal editors and reviewers use criteria to evaluate the suitability of the article for publication such as the significance and novelty of the findings, contributions to the field, currency of citations, strength of the argument, and clarity of the writing. Sample questions that reviewers may be asked to comment on are:

Does the paper fit the standards and scope of the journal it is being considered for?

Is the research question clear?

Was the approach appropriate?

Is the study design, methods and analysis appropriate to the question being studied?

Is the study innovative or original?

Does the study challenge existing paradigms or add to existing knowledge?

Does it develop novel concepts?

Does it matter?

Are the methods described clearly enough for other researchers to replicate?

Are the methods of statistical analysis and level of significance appropriate?

Could presentation of the results be improved and do they answer the question?

If humans, human tissues or animals are involved, was ethics approval gained and was the study ethical?

Are the conclusions appropriate?

(From *Peer Review: the nuts and bolts*, http://www.senseaboutscience.org/data/files/resources/99/Peer-review_The-nuts-and-bolts.pdf)

Reviewers read and comment on manuscript submissions as a form of service to the academy; they are not paid for this work. Reviewers tend to be recruited informally; some journals prefer that scholars have published in the journal before becoming peer reviewers, while others have programs to bring in postgraduates or early career scholars as reviewers. In many disciplines a shortage of peer reviewers means that the reviewing process can take a long time (and suggests the need for a larger pool of reviewers – see Chapter 16).

Blinded or masked peer review means that the author's name and identifying information (institution, earlier publications cited) are omitted from the version of the submitted manuscript that reviewers see. The intention with this approach is to reduce potential bias against an author if her identity were to be known; however, as a scholar's work becomes known in a discipline, reviewers may be able to guess at her identity. In some cases, depending on the policies of the journal and the practices of the discipline, reviewers' identities are disclosed along with their reviews.

Double-blind peer review means that both the author's and reviewers' names are kept confidential. As double-blind peer reviewing can be considered a mark of scholarly quality, it is an ISI requirement for journals to be included in its databases, particularly in high-status indexes.

The peer review process is not unproblematic or uncontroversial. Concerns about the potential for bias have led some scholars to call for more transparency about reviewers' identities, to serve as both an accountability measure and a way to enable authors to get assistance from reviewers during the publication trajectory (see Belcher, 2007). Yet, given ISI's requirements for including journals in its indexes, the pressure to maintain the current system continues.

Note

1   This distinction was found to be the case in our research, yet we also know there is a wide range of brokering practices. For a recent volume on the approach of author's editors, see Matarese (2013).

Chapter 15

Communicating with publishing gatekeepers

15.1 **Chapter focus**

Getting published involves engaging in a number of communication practices that include – and go beyond – writing a journal article. Effective communication with gatekeepers such as journal editors, both before and after submission of your article, can be crucial to ensuring publishing success. Communication with gatekeepers may begin in the cover letter written to accompany a manuscript and continue through postal, email or online correspondence about revisions to an article. Understanding how to approach communication and respond to editors' and reviewers' correspondence and reviews can help you understand the revisions that a journal's editors and reviewers have requested or suggested, whether and how to make such revisions, and how to communicate to the journal editor about the changes you make. In this chapter we examine how scholars approach this important – and sometimes under-appreciated – practice of academic publishing.

15.2 **Guidelines for authors from two journals**

In this section we examine guidelines to authors for submitting manuscripts from the two psychology journals discussed in Chapter 5. Look at the guidelines presented in Data Example 15.1 and consider these questions: How do these instructions compare to each other? How do they address the concerns of writers who use English as an additional language?

Data Example 15.1: Instructions for authors from two journals

Instructions for authors from the APA

As noted, *Psychological Review* is published by the American Psychological Association (APA), whose guidelines for authors are shared across the association's publications.

Prior to submission, please carefully read and follow the submission guidelines detailed below. Manuscripts that do not conform to the submission guidelines may be returned without review.

General correspondence may be directed to the Editor's office.

Do not submit manuscripts to the Editor's email address.

All submissions should be clear and readable. An unusual typeface is acceptable only if it is clear and legible.

In addition to addresses and phone numbers, please supply electronic mail addresses and fax numbers, if available, for potential use by the editorial office and later by the production office.

Masked Review Policy

Masked review is optional for this journal. Include authors' names and affiliations only in the cover letter for the manuscript. Authors who desire masked review should make every effort to see that the manuscript itself contains no clues to their identities.

Manuscript Preparation

Prepare manuscripts according to the *Publication Manual of the American Psychological Association* (6th edition). Manuscripts may be copyedited for bias-free language (see Chapter 3 of the *Publication Manual*).

Review APA's Checklist for Manuscript Submission before submitting your article.

If your manuscript was mask reviewed, please ensure that the final version for production includes a byline and full author note for typesetting.

Double-space all copy. Other formatting instructions, as well as instructions on preparing tables, figures, references, metrics, and abstracts, appear in the *Manual*.

Instructions for authors from *Learning and Instruction*

NEW: Peer Review Policy for Learning and Instruction

The practice of peer review plays a vital role in maintaining the high standards of *Learning and Instruction*. All manuscripts are peer reviewed following the procedure outlined below.

Initial Manuscript Evaluation

The Editor first evaluates all manuscripts. Manuscripts rejected at this stage have a poor structure, serious scientific flaws, or are outside the aims and scope of the journal. Manuscripts that meet the minimum criteria are normally passed on to three experts for review. Authors of manuscripts rejected at this stage will usually be informed within 14 days of receipt.

Type of Peer Review

Learning and Instruction employs double blind reviewing, where both the referee and author remain anonymous throughout the process.

How the Referee is Selected

Referees are matched to the paper according to their expertise. Our database is constantly being updated.

Referee Reports

Referees are asked to evaluate whether:

- The manuscript contributes significantly to the development of research in the domain.
- The research issue/problem is clearly introduced.
- The theoretical presentation is relevant to the problem.
- The method and analysis are sound.
- The results are described in an appropriate way.
- The interpretation and discussion of results is well founded.

Language correction is not part of the peer review process, but referees may suggest corrections to the manuscript. In order to assure comprehensibility and quality of the submission, authors who are not native English speakers or very proficient are strongly encouraged to have their manuscript corrected by a native English speaker.

How long does the review process take?

The time required for the review process is dependent on the response of the referees. However, the typical time for *Learning and Instruction* is approximately 6-10 weeks. Revised manuscripts might be returned to the initial referees who may then request another revision of a manuscript.

Authors' Response to Editor and Reviewers

The submission of a revised version of a manuscript should be accompanied by a letter detailing each of the changes the authors have made in response to reviewers' and editor's comments and recommendations. All reviewers' comments and recommendations should be reported in this letter, followed by the authors' response with reference to the number of the page in which a required change appears on the revised version.

The Editor's decision is final

Referees advise the Editor, who is responsible for the final decision to accept or reject the article. The Editor's decision will be sent to the author with all recommendations made by the referees.

Comment

*The author guidelines for **Psychological Review** (PR) are relatively brief, as the notes refer authors to related topics on the APA website. Possibly because **PR** is published in the United States, where the assumption is that publishing takes place in English by users of English as a first language, the journal's guidelines do not address language brokering. In contrast, the more robust **Learning & Instruction** (L&I) guidelines explain the review process, criteria that peer reviewers use and a rough timeframe. The guidelines also recognize that manuscripts may come from multilingual authors who may wish to use language brokering, here called 'language correction'. (See Lillis and Curry [2010, Chapter 6] for ideologies of language brokering.)*

15.3 **Preparing a manuscript for submission**

Scholars approach the preparation and submission of manuscripts in different ways. Consider Julie's account in Data Example 15.2 of preparing a manuscript for a specific journal and consider these questions: How early in the process of writing does Julie examine the journals she may want to target? What aspects does she focus on when preparing a manuscript?

Data Example 15.2: Understanding the requirements of specific journals

Julie, associate professor, education, Hungary

'I wouldn't submit anything if I'm not aware of what they expect in terms of content. I always look at the journal, what they have published before in terms of content and when I write the article I actually write it with having the requirements in front of me, what kind of citation style, because sometimes journals require a different citation style from APA, or what headings they would need or table formatting and these kinds of things.'

Comment

Julie establishes from the start – and is confident by the time she submits – that her paper connects with the various conversations of the journal. However, she also pays careful attention to aspects that can sometimes be considered less important, such as the conventions that the journal values set out in the submission guidelines (the 'requirements'). These include formatting and layout and referencing style (e.g. APA). By consulting the guidelines at multiple points in writing and preparing her manuscript, Julie aims to ensure that her paper will meet the requirements and thus be considered an appropriate submission by the editor who first screens it.

15.4 Attaching a cover letter

Data Example 15.3 presents a scholar's letter accompanying a submission. Read it and consider these questions: Why do you think this scholar gave the word count and summary of findings? What other information could the author include?

Data Example 15.3: Extracts from a journal submission cover letter

[Name], Editor

[Journal Title]

Dear Professor [Editor's name],

Please find enclosed a copy of our article entitled [title of article]. The article is 9234 words long and is intended to be a research article. The main findings of our study are that [description of findings]. We hope that our paper will be of interest for your journal.

Yours sincerely,

[Name]

[Title]

[Department]

[University], [Location]

Comment

As the author guidelines presented in Data Example 15.1 illustrate, journals often limit the length of submissions, so including a word count is useful so the editor can know the limit has been observed. Providing a summary of research findings in the cover letter is a quick way to signal how the paper may be appropriate for the journal. Other information to consider including is a statement that the article has not been previously published and is not currently under review elsewhere, and additional author names and affiliations. If the research is funded by a grant or institution, information about the funding source may also be mentioned.

15.5 **Communicating about revisions**

Data Example 15.4 presents a cover letter for the revised manuscript that Spanish psychology scholar Carla sent to the second journal in the text history discussed in Chapter 8. Look over the letter and consider these questions: How does Carla present the changes and structure her comments? How does she handle disagreements with the reviewers?

Dear [Editor]:

The manuscript [title] by [Carla and co-author] has been revised according to the suggestions made by the reviewers. I enclose a new version of the original manuscript incorporating them.

The major changes include the addition of a table (table 1) summarizing part of the results of the ANOVA analysis, according to the suggestions made by reviewer B. The other modifications and responses to the reviewer are detailed below.

I hope that with these modifications the paper can be considered for publication in [journal name].

Sincerely,

[Carla]

Reviewer A

I appreciate the careful review of all typing and style errors. All of them have been corrected:

Abstract: lines 5-8

Page 6, line 5-8

Page 8, Section 3. Results: line 3

Page 10, last three lines

Page 14, line 7

Page 16, line 15-16

Page 18, Section 7. Discussion: line 1

Page 19, lines 6 and 5 from the bottom

Page 20, line 14

Page 7, A. Stimuli, line 3-4

The new version of the paper explains better which [data] were used in the experiment by including [...] symbols.

Line 5-11

The [data] were adjusted [according to the reviews]. As reviewer A points out, this means that [result]. However, as the task [X] was to recognize [X] I think that the results of the experiment will not be significantly altered by this fact. [...] However, I think this does not affect significantly the conclusions of the experiment whose objective is [X].

Reviewer B

Page 9, line 10-16

Page 10, line 1-6

Page 10, last paragraph

Page 11, line 14-20

These statistical results of the ANOVAS, made for each [data point] are presented in a table in the new version.

[additional discussion] I agree with reviewer B that the role of [data] should be included. So, the revised version of the paper includes this explanation.

[Additional comments about revisions]

Comment

Carla's cover letter summarizes the main changes she has made, then addresses the concerns of each reviewer, noting the manuscript page numbers on which she made changes. She also states where she disagrees with reviewers and gives reasons. Responding to reviewers' comments can be challenging, particularly if reviewers contradict each other. In such cases it is even more crucial to set out clearly in a cover letter which of the reviewers' positions you have accepted in the revision; if you have questions about whether to reject a reviewer's suggestions or how to handle conflicting suggestions, you can contact the editor for clarification. In fact, most editors have experience with such communication and welcome your engagement in the process by asking such questions.

15.6 **Thinking about your practice**

1. If you have not already submitted an article for publication, where might you find the information you need about journal requirements?

2. Are there particular journals' requirements or conventions that you find problematic and, if so, how might you deal with this?

3. If you receive confusing or contradictory reviewer comments, who might you discuss such comments with in order to revise your paper?

15.7 **Suggestions for future action**

1. Use the website of journals that you are interested in to locate the guidelines for authors and review policies.

2. Consider asking colleagues for samples of their correspondence with journals if you are unsure about appropriate form or content.

3. When reviews and correspondence arrive from a journal editor you can make a table with each of the editor's and reviewers' comments in one column, your plans for revision in another column and any questions for the editor in a third column. Consider who might be available to help you interpret and respond to the feedback, particularly if it is contradictory or the editor's letter or decision is confusing.

15.8 **Useful resources**

- Mediterranean Editors and Translators is an association of language service providers. Their website offers a range of resources, including a list of organizations in different parts of the world that offer support in writing for publication: http://www.metmeetings.org/en/links:584.

- Swales, J. and Feak, C. (2011) *Navigating Academia: Writing Supporting Genres.* Ann Arbor: University of Michigan Press, includes a chapter, 'Supporting the publication process,' on submitting manuscripts, writing biographical statements to accompany an article, and writing acknowledgments.

- The American Psychological Association (2010) *Publication Manual* (6th edn). Washington, DC: Author, includes a section, 'Preparing the manuscript for submission', discussing the order of pages in a manuscript, how to submit supplemental materials, and what to include in a cover letter. It also includes a Checklist for Manuscript Submission (Section 8.07).

- Belcher, W. (2009) *Writing Your Journal Article in 12 Weeks: A Guide to Academic Publishing Success.* Thousand Oaks, CA: Sage, Chapter 12, 'Sending your article!,' discusses formatting the article according to the journal's style, preparing illustrations, and writing a cover letter. Her last chapter, 'Responding to journal decisions', explains the types of decisions gatekeepers make and offers advice on responding to feedback.

- Paltridge, B. and S. Starfield (in press) *Getting Published in Academic Journals: Navigating the Publication Process.* Ann Arbor: University of Michigan Press. This workbook focuses on responding to editors' and reviewers' feedback on manuscripts submitted for publication.

15.9 **Related research**

- Cheung, Y.L. (2010) First publications in refereed English journals: Difficulties, coping strategies, and recommendations for student training. *System,* 38, 134-141. This interview study of six applied linguistics PhD students in Hong Kong explores how they approached writing for publication and the feedback they got from journal editors.

- Sionis, C. (1995) Communication strategies in the writing of scientific research articles by non-native users of English. *English for Specific Purposes* 14 (2), 99-113. This comparative study of two generations of French scholars writing for publication in English found generational differences in attitudes toward language learning that manifested in scholars' writing strategies and publishing success rates.

Information Box 15: Online submissions systems

Many publishers use online journal submissions systems that have replaced the older procedure of sending multiple copies of a manuscript by post or the more recent practice of submitting manuscripts by electronic mail directly to the journal editor. Online systems enable authors, journal editors and reviewers to access manuscript submissions and interact with each other electronically. These systems provide a record of when a manuscript was submitted and acted upon, which can be helpful if your manuscript has been under review for a long time (depending on journal and discipline, three to six months may be a typical wait before you get a journal's decision and/or referees' reports). These systems may also allow reviewers to access the reviews and the editor's decision about a manuscript.

Some journals use commercial systems such as ScholarOne™ or Manuscript Central™, while others connected to large publishing companies use that company's own system (e.g. Elsevier). A portal on the journal webpage (usually on the publisher's website) leads to the online system where an author can set up an account for submitting manuscripts and check on their progress (see Information Box 6 for timelines). Guidelines for submitting manuscripts electronically are also provided on journal webpages – often the cover page of a manuscript with information identifying the author(s) is uploaded separately, as are the title and abstract page, figures and tables and other ancillary components. If you have difficulty in accessing the system (because of poor Internet connectivity in your region or other technical issues), contact the editor directly by electronic mail for help.

Chapter 16

Producing a journal: Taking on reviewing and editing roles

16.1 **Chapter focus**

Scholarly journals are considered one of the most important ways of sharing and distributing knowledge around the world. At different career moments, scholars take on a variety of roles related to academic knowledge production through publishing. Playing a role in editorial decision-making through peer reviewing journal submissions, serving on an editorial board and editing a journal are key ways of shaping scholarly conversations globally. While these tasks entail considerable time and commitment, they contribute in important ways to shaping not just the conversations in a particular field of knowledge but also the decisions about who can get access to which conversations, including the language(s) or varieties of languages articles may be submitted and published in and whether a journal is open access or 'restricted'.

16.2 **Reviewing manuscripts for publication**

Many journal websites provide guidelines for becoming a reviewer, as illustrated in Data Example 16.1, which comes from one of the journals examined earlier in the guide. Read the guidelines and answer this question: According to the journal, what benefits do reviewers gain by performing this service?

Data Example 16.1: From 'Becoming a referee for *Learning and Instruction*'

If you are not currently a referee for *Learning and Instruction* but would like to be considered as a referee, please contact the editorial office at: jli@ elsevier.com. The benefits of refereeing for *Learning and Instruction* include the opportunity to read, see, and evaluate the latest work in your research area at an early stage, and to contribute to the overall integrity of scientific research and its published documentation. You will also be acknowledged in an annual statement in *Learning and Instruction*. Reviewers who provide their reports using the Elsevier Editorial System (EES) also receive a month's free access to SCOPUS (www.scopus.com), the world's largest abstracting and indexing database, for every review provided. You may also be able to cite your work for *Learning and Instruction* as part of your professional development requirements for various professional societies and organizations.

Comment

In this extract the journal identifies the benefits of becoming a reviewer as: taking part in the larger knowledge-making practices of one's discipline, getting free access to a material resource, the SCOPUS database, and receiving public recognition for the work that reviewers do by being included in the annual listing of reviewers in the journal. As the website notes, the work of reviewing can also be counted as professional service and scholars typically include this service in annual institutional reports on their work. However, whilst journals do have open calls for reviewers, as in the example above, scholars are often invited to become reviewers through contacts they have established via other means. For example, sometimes after publishing an article in a journal, scholars are invited to become reviewers; scholars are sometimes contacted after presenting at a conference; or post-graduate supervisors may be contacted by a journal to recommend students and early career colleagues to become reviewers. Increasingly, journal editors are searching the Internet to find appropriate reviewers, so you may be contacted, for example, on the basis of information on your web page.

16.3 **Additional benefits of reviewing manuscripts**

Reviewing is one means of forging disciplinary conversations. It also has the advantage of offering writers deeper insights into the range of linguistic and rhetorical practices in academic writing. Hungarian psychology scholar Gyorgy has served as a reviewer of manuscripts submitted to Hungarian-medium journals since 1995 and to English-medium journals since 2001. Read his comment on these experiences and answer this question: What kinds of knowledge has Gyorgy gained by reviewing manuscripts by other scholars?

Data Example 16.2: Learning from reviewing

Gyorgy, professor, psychology, Hungary

'First, I realized how short and expressively native American and English authors write the introduction of their papers. This is quite complicated for me – we, in Hungary, have got used to writing long introductions with all the related knowledge. Second, noticing the failures of statistical analyses in the other authors' papers is much easier than in our own and these experiences can be used in my work.'

Comment

Serving as a reviewer highlighted both content and stylistic issues for Gyorgy. For him, the experience of reviewing emphasised some common stylistic differences between Anglophone writers' article introductions and those written – in this case – by Hungarian scholars. With regard to content, the deeper awareness that Gyorgy developed of the methodological shortcomings evident in others' papers has benefitted his own academic writing.

16.4 **Taking on editorial roles: Decisions and choices**

It is calculated that some 50,000 academic journals are currently being published in a large range of languages. The 11 most commonly used languages are English, Mandarin Chinese, Hindi/Urdu, Spanish, Arabic, Russian, Portuguese, Bengali, French, Japanese and German (Lillis & Curry, 2010). All of these journals need editors in order to survive and grow. Scholars are therefore faced with considerable choice and sometimes difficult decisions about which journals to concentrate their energies on, not only as authors but also as reviewers and editors. Read the extracts in Data Example 16.3 and consider the types of journals that scholars have decided to work on as editors. What do you notice about the journals' goals and the interests of the scholars in being editors?

Data Example 16.3: Editing different types of journals

Journal 1: Interest in research methodologies

Margarida is the editor of a Portuguese journal which has been in existence for some six years. It publishes articles and research notes, reviews and theoretical discussions, but has the explicit goal of publishing papers with a specific focus on experimental methodologies. A further explicitly stated goal is to publish papers on research methodologies being developed in Portugal that are being used with Portuguese-speaking populations. Margarida considers that the journal is important for many reasons, including the need to sustain and to develop a specialist scientific discourse in Portuguese, which she sees as central to building a strong national research community. Whilst the work of editing the journal is considerable, Margarida receives high praise from colleagues for taking on this endeavor and she also regularly receives positive comments from students who are pleased to be able to access current research in the medium of Portuguese.

Journal 2: Interest in transdisciplinarity

Gejza is on the editorial board of a Central European journal which has a specific transdisciplinary framing, which means that it is interested in contributions which cross specialist boundaries. The journal has a history of some 20 years. It currently only publishes English-medium articles but offers a translation service for articles submitted in Slovak and Czech. Gejza has a longstanding commitment to this journal because he considers it an important way of presenting and sharing research and theory from the local national context with scholars around the world as well as opening up new lines of intellectual inquiry transnationally. The journal has been through several stages in terms of its key goals and currently is seeking to be included in the SSCI as part of establishing itself as an 'international' journal.

Journal 3: Interest in multilingual publishing

Andrés, an associate professor of psychology in Spain, is the editor of a recently established open access journal which accepts and publishes submissions in five languages. The five working languages of the journal reflect the languages that members of the editorial board know and that reviewers can read and offer reviews on. Andrés was encouraged by his department to set up a journal, with one goal being to make the work of the department more visible. He considers the journal to be a success in that papers are regularly being submitted, reviewed and published and that the journal seems to be increasing the department's visibility in a specific academic field.

Comment

Journals obviously differ in terms of the disciplinary fields they cover. But as the examples illustrate, they differ in other important ways. They may have different overarching goals with regard to fields of knowledge; we see that Journal 1 is concerned with one specialist aspect of a field, in contrast to Journal 2, which is challenging disciplinary boundaries and opening up disciplinary frames of reference. Another key difference is in the languages used: Journal 1 is published in the local/national language (Portuguese) and its production practices – including reviewing – take place in that language; Journal 2 publishes in English but accepts submissions in some local and regional languages and offers some support for translation; Journal 3 publishes in five languages, with reviews being carried out in those languages. And there are specific reasons for the different decisions around which languages should be used. Journal 1 explicitly seeks to publish research in the national language in order to sustain national research capacity and knowledge making. Journal 2 publishes in English with the aim of making research carried out in the local contexts (and languages) more available to scholars outside these contexts. This journal has also taken the decision to publish in English because – given the global status of English – it considers using English as the best way of opening up a new area of inquiry internationally. Journal 3 publishes in five languages in recognition that research is being carried out and produced in those languages and that it therefore makes sense for articles to be published in those languages.

Editing a journal involves considerable effort and time. Scholars – as in the examples above – choose to become editors of particular journals for academic motives (e.g. to develop a particular area of knowledge) and a range of personal and ideological reasons (e.g. to maintain local research capacity and/or to sustain knowledges in a range of languages and/or to facilitate transnational exchange[1]). In addition, editing a journal is generally considered to be a prestigious role in academia, with attendant institutional rewards (and in some cases materials support for the work).

16.5 Thinking about your practice

1. Have you reviewed articles, conference presentation proposals/abstracts, grant applications, or other texts submitted for evaluation? Do you know anyone in your context who does reviewing?

2. Are you involved in the production of scholarly journals in your context or transnationally? What roles have you played and which might you like to take on?

3. What challenges do you face in reviewing and/or editing and where can you find guidance and advice on these important roles?

16.6 Suggestions for future action

1. Identify the journals that you read on a regular basis and/or that you want to publish in. Check the journal's website for the list of editor(s), editorial board members and their institutions to see if you are familiar with their work. Does your work contribute to the conversations that the editors and board members of the journal are interested in?

2. Discuss with colleagues and/or supervisors whether you should contact a particular journal's editor to discuss becoming a reviewer (some journals welcome both experienced scholars and advanced postgraduates).

3. Consider whether anyone in your local institution or context is working on the production of an academic journal that you might like to assist with or who might be able to give you information about helping to produce a journal.

16.7 **Useful resources**

- The website GradShare includes a page on how to become a journal reviewer (http://www.gradshare.com/advice.html?id=631; accessed 11 August 2013).

- The American Psychological Association provides 'A graduate student's guide to involvement in the peer review process' (http://www.apa.org/ research/publishing/peer-review.pdf; accessed 11 March 2013).

- The journal *Nature* offers a blog on peer reviewing (Peer to Peer), which includes this entry: http://blogs.nature.com/peer-to-peer/2009/09/ becoming_a_peerreviewer_for_a.html (accessed 11 August 2013).

- Mullen, C.A. (2011) Journal editorship: Mentoring, democratic, and international perspectives. *The Educational Forum*, 75, 328-42.

16.8 **Related research**

- Tardy, C. and Matsuda, P. (2009) The construction of author voice by editorial board members. *Written Communication* 26 (1), 32-52. Reports on a survey of 70 editorial board members of six journals in applied linguistics and writing studies, showing that even in blind peer review referees construct a notion of the author's identity, which may cause them to focus on certain aspects of the writing over others.

- Hewings, M. (2006) English language standards in academic articles: Attitudes of peer reviewers. *Revista Canaria de Estudios Ingleses* 53, 47-62. Findings of this study of 228 peer reviews of articles submitted to *English for Specific Purposes Journal* show that while reviewers made more negative comments on papers written by users of English as an additional language compared with 'native' English speakers, other factors such as fit with the journal's goals need to be considered in understanding reviewers' evaluations.

Information Box 16: Journal mentoring programmes

In addition to their gatekeeping role – as reviewers and editors – members of editorial boards may provide informal support or 'mentoring' for writers. This may take place even when – or especially when – a paper is being rejected. In fact, an editor or a reviewer may take the time to give considerable feedback on a rejected paper in order to help support the writer's future efforts. More formal types of mentoring also exist whereby an editorial board offers specific advice on how to write for their journal. A good example of this is the approach adopted for some time by the *Croatian Medical Journal*, a high status journal published in English in Croatia. Acknowledging the challenges that multilingual writers in particular face, the journal's editors developed what they refer to as 'an instructional editorial policy' whereby they give considerable support to writers in the pre-review period. Before papers are submitted for formal review they offer support on four areas they see as key to a successful paper: the quality of the study, the narrative, the scientific reporting style and the language (Mišak, Marušić & Marušić, 2005).

Anglophone-centre journals are also increasingly aware of the challenges and obstacles faced by scholars working outside of the centre in languages other than English and the importance of taking a more proactive stance towards supporting writers in order to facilitate global scientific exchange (see Mullen, 2011). Some journals are beginning to develop mentoring programmes for writers who are planning to submit an article to their journal, but may be unfamiliar with the conversations of that journal or may need support in drafting an English-medium paper. One such mentoring programme – attached to an international journal, *Compare* – has been running for several years. The programme is advertised via the professional organization associated with the journal. Authors are encouraged to apply if they have not previously published in *Compare*. In this programme writers have two types of mentors: academic mentors who focus on the content and language mentors who focus on language. Whilst in practice the work of these two types of mentors overlaps, writers have valued the two kinds of emphasis in commentary and feedback (Lillis, Magyar & Robinson-Pant, 2010, 2013).

The core features of the mentoring programme are:
- A workshop given the day before a key relevant academic conference;
- Opportunities during the day workshop to give detailed attention to texts – by reading and discussing specific text histories from *Compare*'s archives; (Permission is sought from authors and reviewers for such use.)
- Email support to authors by academic and writing mentors;
- Email support to academic mentors by one of the programme facilitators;

- Email support to authors by the facilitators;
- Structured feedback sheets for use by authors, academic mentors and writing mentors, where considered relevant.

After taking part in the programme, authors submit their papers which are reviewed in the usual way. For guidelines on how to set up a journal mentoring programme and sample resources, see: https://sites.google.com/site/mentoringforpublication. (Accessed 10 August 2013.)

For an example of a different kind of mentoring provided by a journal, see: http://www.technorhetoric.net/board.html; http://lsf.lifescifeed.com/editorial%20board.htm. (Accessed 11 August 2013.)

Note

1   This is a highly complex situation and scholars, editors and journals make specific decisions with regard to the linguistic medium of a journal for a range of reasons. For further discussion, see Lillis (2012).

Chapter 17

Concluding thoughts – critical choices and practical strategies for global scholarly publishing

The practices of global academic publishing are changing rapidly, creating challenges and tensions for scholars worldwide. Multilingual scholars face particular challenges as they often have to make difficult decisions about which communities to engage with, by means of which publications, in which language(s) and when and in which genres. In this guide we have aimed to illustrate the nature of some of these key challenges by offering authentic accounts of experiences and decisions made by multilingual scholars working with and through several languages on a regular basis. We have pointed to a number of challenges, including scholars' desires to have their work reach the broadest possible audiences or, in some cases, to reach specialized audiences that may be small in authors' contexts. At the same time scholars often must act in response to pressures to publish in English-medium journals, including at moments when scholars may not feel that those outlets are the most appropriate for their work. Many scholars are deeply vested in creating local research cultures and thus worried about pressures and trends that shift the focus – and related resources – away from local communities to support externally imposed goals of increasing a department's, institution's or nation's rankings in terms of research productivity.

Our overarching goal in this guide has been to draw on scholars' experiences to support readers in reflecting on and understanding these practices in order to make more informed choices about writing and publishing that may align with personal interests as well as finding ways to respond to institutional pressures. An additional goal in writing this guide is to open up debate about the nature of the practices in which we are all expected to engage. We think it is important to bring individual scholars' opinions, choices and strategies to bear on current debates about knowledge production, particularly about the role of English in the global academic marketplace and, more specifically, the growing dominance of journal and citation indexes such as the Science and Social Science Citation Indexes (and the impact factor) in regulating which journals are considered worthwhile outlets for scholarly publication. Indeed, within broader discussions about knowledge production that often uncritically promulgate the belief that English is currently an 'academic lingua franca', it is crucial to bring to light the tensions and burdens experienced by multilingual scholars – as well as their/our agency in the face of these pressures.

In this regard, it is worth noting an example of critical resistance to pressures for scholars to publish in English-medium journals, particularly those included in US-dominated indexes. This resistance is illustrated by a campaign in Taiwan, where more than 2000 academics mainly from the social sciences supported a public petition launched against government policies that, among other things, reward publications in journals included in the Science and Social Science Citation Indexes more than publications in other journals. As a news report stated, 'Some scholars [. . .] believe that using publication in academic journals of science, such as SSCI and SCI, as evaluation criterion is a form of "self-colonization" by adopting the criterion from the western countries' ('Academia is launching …', *United Evening News*, December 28, 2010). Scholars proposed alternative criteria for evaluation which include publishing books, presenting at conferences and engaging in other scholarly activities in addition to publishing journal articles. While it is difficult to say what may be the results of such efforts, it is important to be aware of the fact that scholars are actively challenging what they perceive to be inappropriate and unrealistic demands.

In addition, as noted in the Introduction, the growing open access movement has resulted from an international campaign to provide alternatives to currently restricted access to global knowledge circulation through open access journals and repositories. The 'open access' movement aims to support the free circulation of knowledge globally, working against the increasingly high subscription costs for journals, particularly those distributed by commercial publishers. As articulated by the Budapest Open Access Initiative:

> By 'open access' we mean free availability [of research] on the public internet, permitting any users to read, download, copy, distribute, print, search, or link to the full texts of these articles, trawl them for indexing, pass them as data to software, or use them for any other lawful purpose, without financial, legal, or technical barriers other than those inseparable from gaining access to the internet itself. (Open Society Institute, 2002)[1]

The number of freely available open access journals is growing quickly (for a directory, see http://doaj.org).[2] Among the journals included in Ulrichsweb.com (discussed in Chapter 1), 7472 are listed as both open access and peer reviewed (as of February 2013). 'Open access' is also being enacted at informal levels, where scholars globally – increasingly aware of the inequalities surrounding publishing – are making available drafts of articles, published articles, and even whole books, on their personal webpages or in institutional repositories. These efforts at increasing access challenge the corporate model of knowledge dissemination in which research is a commodity to be purchased (for discussion see Salager-Meyer, 2012). While a predatory group of open access publishers has also emerged (Beall, 2013), it is important not to lose sight of the aims of the work of the Budapest Open Access Initiative and others to support the free and open circulation of academic knowledge worldwide.

In closing, we hope that this guide will prove useful to scholars in navigating the complex world of writing for academic publication whilst it contributes to debates about the nature of this world, what it is and what we might want it to be.

Notes

1   For fuller discussion see Lillis and Curry (2010), Chapter 7.

2   The Directory of Open Access Repositories is found at http://www.opendoar.org/index.html. As document repositories do not evaluate the texts they include, they are not generally considered to be peer reviewed sites. For examples of document repositories see https://ur-research.rochester.edu/home.action and http://oro.open.ac.uk/. Scholars in the open access movement have created the categories of 'Gold' and 'Green' access, with Gold referring to open access journals and Green referring to repositories. According to Pinfield (2009), open access journals and repositories are not two distinct ways to access journal articles, but rather, some repositories and OA journals interact with each other.

References

'Academia is launching a movement against academic hegemony', (December 28, 2010) *United Evening News*, Taiwan.

Agre, P. (2002) *Networking on the Network: A Guide to Professional Skills for PhD Students*, accessed 06 June 2012. http://vlsicad.ucsd.edu/Research/Advice/network.html.

American Psychological Association (2010) *Publication Manual* (6th edn). Washington, DC: Author.

Bazerman, C. (1980) A relationship between reading and writing: The conversational model. *College English* 41, 656-61.

Beall, J. (2013) *Beall's List of Predatory, Open-access Publishers*, accessed 10 August 2013. https://www.facebook.com/POA.Publishers.

Belcher, D. (2007) Seeking acceptance in an English-only research world. *Journal of Second Language Writing* 16 (1), 1-22.

Belcher, D. and Connor, U. (eds) (2001) *Reflections on Multiliterate Lives*. Clevedon: Multilingual Matters.

Belcher, W. (2009) *Writing Your Journal Article in 12 Weeks: A Guide to Academic Publishing Success*. Thousand Oaks, CA: Sage.

Boden, R., Kenway, J. and Epstein, D. (2007) *Building Networks*. London: SAGE.

Bucholtz, M. (2000) The politics of transcription. *Journal of Pragmatics* 32 (10), 1439-1465.

Canagarajah, A.S. (1996) Nondiscursive requirements in academic publishing, material resources of periphery scholars, and the politics of knowledge production. *Written Communication* 13 (4), 435-472.

Canagarajah, A.S. (2002) *A Geopolitics of Academic Writing*. Pittsburgh: University of Pittsburgh Press.

Casanave, C.P. (2002) *Writing Games: Multicultural case studies of academic literacy practices in higher education*. Mahwah, NJ: Lawrence Erlbaum.

Casanave, C.P. and Li, X. (eds) (2008) *Learning the Literacy Practices of Graduate School: Insiders' reflections on academic enculturation*. Ann Arbor: University of Michigan Press.

Casanave, C.P. and Vandrick, S. (2003) *Writing for Scholarly Publication: Behind the Scenes in Language Education*. Mahwah, NJ: Lawrence Erlbaum.

Carnell, E., MacDonald, J., McCallum, B. and Scott, M. (2008) *Passion and Politics: Academics Reflect on Writing for Publication*. London: Institute of Education.

Curry, M.J. and Lillis, T. (2004) Multilingual scholars and the imperative to publish in English: Negotiating interests, demands, and rewards. *TESOL Quarterly* 38 (4), 663-688.

Curry, M.J. and Lillis, T. (2010a) Academic research networks: Accessing resources for English-medium publishing. *English for Specific Purposes* 29, 281-295.

Curry, M.J. and Lillis, T. (2010b) Making academic publishing practices visible: Designing research-based heuristics to support English-medium text production. In N. Harwood (ed.) *Language Teaching Materials: Theory and Practice* (pp. 322-345). Cambridge: Cambridge University Press.

Defazio, D., Lockett, A. and Wright, M. (2009) Funding incentives, collaborative dynamics and scientific productivity: Evidence from the EU framework program. *Research Policy* 38, 293-305.

Feak, C. and Swales, J. (2011) *Creating Contexts: Writing Introductions Across Genres*. Ann Arbor: University of Michigan Press.

Flowerdew, J. (1999a) Writing for scholarly publication in English: The case of Hong Kong. *Journal of Second Language Writing* 8 (2), 123-45.

— (1999b) Problems in writing for scholarly publication in English: The case of Hong Kong. *Journal of Second Language Writing* 8 (3), 243-64.

— (2000) Discourse community, legitimate peripheral participation, and the nonnative-English-speaking scholar. *TESOL Quarterly* 34 (1), 127-50.

Giltrow, J. (2002) *Academic Writing: Writing and Reading in the Disciplines* (3rd edn). Peterborough, Canada: Broadview Press.

Graff, G. and Birkenstein, C. (2010) *They Say, I Say: The Moves That Matter in Academic Writing* (2nd edn). New York/London: Norton.

Henson, K.T. (2005) *Writing for Publication: Road to Academic Advancement.* Boston, MA: Allyn & Bacon.

International Committee of Medical Journal Editors (1984) Style matters: Multiple publication. *British Medical Journal* 288, 52.

Katz, J.S. and Martin, B. (1997) What is research collaboration? *Research Policy* 26, 1-18.

Lillis, T. (2008) Ethnography as method, methodology and 'deep theorising': Closing the gap between text and context in academic writing research. *Written Communication* 25 (3), 353-388.

Lillis, T. (2012) Economies of signs in writing for academic publication: The case of English medium 'national' journals. *Journal of Advanced Composition* 32 (3-4), 695-722.

Lillis, T.M. and Curry, M.J. (2006a) Professional academic writing by multilingual scholars: Interactions with literacy brokers in the production of English-medium texts. *Written Communication* 23 (1), 3-35.

Lillis, T.M. and Curry, M.J. (2006b) Reframing notions of competence in scholarly writing: From individual to networked activity. *Revista Canaria de Estudios Ingleses* 53, 63-78.

Lillis, T.M. and Curry, M.J. (2010) *Academic Writing in a Global Context: The Politics and Practices of Publishing in English.* London: Routledge.

Lillis, T.M. and Curry, M.J. (2013) English, scientific publishing and participation in the global knowledge economy. In E. Erling and P. Seargeant (eds) *English and International Development* (pp. 220-242). Bristol: Multilingual Matters.

Lillis, T., Hewings, A., Vladimirou, D. and Curry, M.J. (2010) The geolinguistics of English as an Academic Lingua Franca: Citation practices across English medium national and English medium international journals. *International Journal of Applied Linguistics* 20 (1), 111-135.

Lillis, T., Magyar, A. and Robinson-Pant, A. (2010) An international journal's attempts to address inequalities in academic publishing: Developing writing for publication programme. *Compare: A Journal of Comparative and International Education* 40 (6), 781-800.

Lillis, T., Magyar, A. and Robinson-Pant, A. (2013) Putting 'wordface' work at the centre of academic text production: Working with an international journal to develop an authors' mentoring programme. In V. Materese (ed.) *Supporting Research Writing: Roles and Challenges in Multilingual Settings* (pp. 237-255). Cambridge, UK: Chandos Publishing.

Lunsford, A. and Ede, L. (2012) *Writing Together: Collaboration in Theory and Practice.* New York: Bedford/St. Martin's Press.

Materese, V. (ed.) (2013) *Supporting Research Writing: Roles and Challenges in Multilingual Settings.* Cambridge, UK: Chandos Publishing.

Melin, G. (2000) Pragmatism and self-organization: Research collaboration at the individual level. *Research Policy* 29, 31-40.

Mišak, A., Marušić, M. and Marušić, A. (2005) Manuscript editing as a way of teaching academic writing: Experience from a small scientific journal. *Journal of Second Language Writing* 14, 122-131.

Mullen, C.A. (2011) Journal editorship: Mentoring, democratic, and international perspectives. *The Educational Forum* 75 (4), 328-342.

Murray, R. (2009) *Writing for Academic Journals* (2nd edn). Berkshire, UK: McGraw Hill/Open University Press.

Mweru, M. (2010) Why Kenyan academics do not publish in international refereed journals. *World Social Science Report: Knowledge Divides* (pp. 110-111). Paris: UNESCO.

Nygaard, L. (2008) *Writing for Scholars: A Practical Guide to Making Sense and Being Heard.* Oslo: Universitetsforlaget/Copenhagen Business School Press/Liber.

Open Society Institute (2002) *Budapest Open Access Initiative,* accessed 05 July 2013. http://www.soros.org/openaccess/read.

Paltridge, B. and Starfield, S. (in press) *Getting Published in Academic Journals: Navigating the Publication Process.* Ann Arbor: University of Michigan Press.

Paré, A. (2010) Slow the presses: Concerns about premature publication. In C. Aitchison, B. Kamler and A. Lee (eds) *Publishing Pedagogies for the Doctorate and Beyond* (pp. 30-46). Abingdon, UK: Routledge.

Pinfield, S. (2009) Journals and repositories: An evolving relationship? *Learned Publishing* 22, 165-75.

Roberts, C. (1997) Transcribing talk: Issues of representation. *TESOL Quarterly* 31 (1), 167-172.

Salager-Meyer, F. (1997) Scientific multilingualism and the 'lesser' languages. *Interciencia* 22 (4), 197-201.

— (2008) Scientific publishing in developing countries: Challenges for the future. *Journal of English for Academic Purposes* 7, 121-132

— (2012) The open access movement or 'edemocracy': Its birth, rise, problems and solutions. *Iberica* 24, 9-28.

Swales, J. (1990) *Genre Analysis: English in Academic and Research Settings.* Cambridge/ New York: Cambridge University Press.

Swales, J. and Feak, C. (2000) *English in Today's Research World: A Writing Guide.* Ann Arbor: University of Michigan Press.

Swales, J. and Feak, C. (2009) *Abstracts and the Writing of Abstracts.* Ann Arbor: University of Michigan Press.

Swales, J. and Feak, C. (2011) *Navigating Academia: Writing Supporting Genres.* Ann Arbor: University of Michigan Press.

Thomson, P. and Kamler, B. (2012) *Writing for Peer Reviewed Journals: Strategies for Getting Published.* London: Routledge.

Uzuner, S. (2008) Multilingual scholars' participation in core/global academic communities: A literature review. *Journal of English for Academic Purposes* 7, 250-263.

van Aalst, J. (2010) Using Google Scholar to estimate the impact of journal articles in education. *Educational Researcher* 39 (5), 387-400.

Wallerstein, I. (1991) *Geopolitics and Geoculture.* Cambridge: Cambridge University Press.

Wen, Q. and Gao, Y. (2007) Dual publication and academic inequality. *International Journal of Applied Linguistics* 17 (2), 221-225.

Wormell, I. (1998) Informetric analysis of the international impact of scientific journals: How 'international' are the international journals? *Journal of Documentation* 54 (5), 584-605.

Index